A COURSE IN FUN WITH
FAST

10 WAYS TO TURN LIFE'S ~~JOURNEY~~ INTO A JOYRIDE

K A R E N   W I A N D

Carlysle & Lloyd Publishing Co., Traverse City, Michigan

Published by
Carlysle & Lloyd Publishing Co.
Traverse City, Michigan

Publisher's Cataloging-in-Publication Data
Wiand, Karen.
Fast Eddie : ten ways to turn life's journey into a joyride / Karen Wiand. –
Traverse City, MI : Carlysle & Lloyd Pub. Co., 2018.

p. ; cm.

ISBN13: 978-0-9980223-0-7

1. Lee, Eddie. 2. Developmentally disabled—United States—Biography. 3.
Happiness. 4. Conduct of life.
I. Title.

HV1570.5.U65 W53 2018
362.1968—dc23   2018942575

Project Coordination by Martha Bullen

Front cover illustration by Patty Eisenbraun
Front cover design by Deana Riddle
Interior design by Deana Riddle, Karen Wiand, and Dennis Wiand
Chapter titles by Fast Eddie

Printed in the United States of America
22   20   19   18   ●   5   4   3   2   1

"**Heartfelt, timely. This book is a beautiful argument for refusing to take life too seriously.** There's something refreshing about unconditional, selfless love. That's Fast Eddie. He brings a peaceful balance to an increasingly off-kilter world."

— **M. Rutledge McCall**, critically acclaimed author

"On Eddie's daily visits to my store, he usually grabs a cup of coffee, announces, 'Uncle Tim, I feel great today' and gives me a big hug. He doesn't know it, but his hugs are as therapeutic to me as my hugs are to him. Knowing Eddie is a blessing. He serves as a reminder to us all that life is to be enjoyed. *A Course in Fun with Fast Eddie* **is a spectacular account of the power of a person's positive attitude.**"

— **Tim Brick**, son of Mary Jean Brick, founder of BrickWays, and owner of BrickWheels in Traverse City, MI

CONTENTS

Fast Eddie -

This book is dedicated to my "Uncle Tim" Brick

Karen -

This is for you, Dad, for teaching us since we were tots to accept and appreciate everyone.

Acknowledgments

A special thank you:

To the families, friends and caregivers of individuals with intellectual disabilities and all special needs who give of themselves every day to make sure their loved one has a home, a voice, and the special care they need and deserve.

To the Brick family for continuing the legacy of Mary Jean's vision that every individual with special needs is included and has an opportunity to live happy and purposeful lives within the community. Because of your work, residents of BrickWays receive the level of support and encouragement they need to live independently.

To Ross and Helen Childs, whose care for their daughter led them to share their strong leadership qualities (Ross is like having Tom Brady in your huddle) and unwavering support to the BrickWays program, providing immeasurable gains for the entire community.

To Patty and Ken Eisenbraun for your infinite generosity, Chandika, from kn literary arts, and Martha Bullen for helping me pull this together.

To Mom and my brothers and sisters.

To Dennis, Kelsey and Dylan.

And a Jeep Wrangler wave to everyone.

INTRODUCTION

It's a Perfect Day for a Joyride

*"If life is a journey, then life's greatest tragedy
is not having enjoyed the trip."*

—1980s BMW Ad

These days, most of us spend a great deal of time catching up on our education. Forget about the years we invest sitting in classrooms; if there is one thing the technology age is teaching us, it's that if we want to remain as functional as our smart phones, we need to plug our adapters in and accept that change is not just the small jingling sound in our pocket after one too many trips to the dollar store. We are constantly reminded that if we don't pick up the pace and respond to every email blast or buy into every proven (but not guaranteed) success program by midnight tonight, we run the risk of missing the boat when our ship comes in.

It's not all bad, since continued learning keeps us in the game; plus, when we think about it, life is an ongoing multiple choice test anyway. It's just that in the midst of all this schooling, there is a lesson that many of us are not grasping. And that's the simple, self-taught concept that we applied as liberally as sunblock to most everything we did when we were knee high to a grasshopper: life is supposed to be fun.

Maybe this is difficult to remember since so many of us are still operating under the influence of our years of formal learning when we were prodded to believe the winning formula has been and always will be: success equals sacrifice plus suffering plus hard work. As problematic as that sounds, we would be hard pressed to accept that if it isn't true, all of our blood and tears have left us with little sweat equity. It seems as we chase after our dreams, our inner child is strapped in the back seat squealing, "Are we close to having fun yet?"

I wrote this book to honor and to share a few secrets from those among us who have a keen sense of what matters most in life and when tested don't need to phone a friend to come up with the winning answer. These gifted individuals are those with intellectual disabilities. Their condition is not a hindrance to their happiness. They have a knack for finding joy in practically everything they do, and they don't waste their energy waiting for better times or conditions in order to feel good.

These special individuals are in touch with their feelings moment to moment and gravitate to doing things in a way that compounds their happiness. I have found that internalizing just a touch of the natural knowhow held by those with developmental disabilities bring opportunities for self-improvement and fulfillment beyond anything I ever could have imagined. By following their lead, we can get back to our roots and remember that happiness is our purpose and the more we feel it, the more we have to share with others.

What accounts for this special knowledge and ability among those with intellectual disabilities? I think it's the fact that these unique individuals don't need to spend time unlearning. Happiness comes easily to them because, unlike so many of us, they haven't learned they can't or shouldn't be happy. They are so comfortable with who they are that they don't need to access self-help books or attend seminars to unravel where things went wrong or to figure out how to get back on track.

They accept who they are, so there's nothing to fix. Then, having never learned the false truth that they need permission to experience happiness, they stay open to experiencing all the wonders the world has to offer. Inasmuch, they accept everyone they meet as a teacher without demanding to see their credentials first. You might say they are sponges among Brillo Pads. I believe these brilliant individuals are angels sent here to remind us that we all have a rightful place in this world and every one of us has something special to offer.

This is the story of Eddie Lee, better known as Fast Eddie, a nickname that has stuck ever since the town barber of Linden used it to praise the way Eddie whizzed around town on and off his bike; it aptly describes the winning attitude Eddie has fostered no matter what life has thrown his way. Despite the heartbreaking reality that his starvation as an infant caused his developmental disability, the subsequent judging and bullying he has endured every year of his life, and his demoralizing experiences in the adult foster care system, he has never stopped believing in himself. He is keenly aware that he is as important as everyone else and that he is just as capable of living on his own terms as everyone else. In spite of his hardships, Eddie's determination to flourish using the tools in his own special toolbox remains intact. In his own unique way, he has taught many people that the world becomes a playground when you show up for your assignment with an open and happy heart.

BE ACTIVE

"Life is like riding a bicycle.
To keep your balance, you must keep moving."

—ALBERT EINSTEIN

It has been said that the people who are meant to be in your life appear, yet we live in such a hyper-connected world that sometimes it seems that we ourselves make people appear. We Google up old flames, hunt down old fishing buddies, or become Facebook friends with people we've never even met just by spending a few seconds online.

Eddie Lee didn't need the Internet to find me. He tapped into a higher frequency to make me reappear. Despite the fact that he lives with a developmental disability, had no family to support him, and was living in a dilapidated adult foster care home in the countryside, Eddie found me using the only search tools he's ever needed—his open heart and his hot rod bike.

In late 2009, I visited Eddie for the first time in more than thirty years. Though we grew up as neighbors in Carson City, Michigan, we'd lost touch in early adulthood. I reconnected with him through my sister, who'd begun sending him boxes of goodies after reading an article about him in *The Flint Journal*. In the article, Eddie was described as being well known and equally well loved throughout the community of Linden, Michigan, where he biked everywhere he went, including to see his mother, who lived at a nursing home in a neighboring town.

The Eddie in the article was the same Eddie I remembered— befriending everyone he met and being honored in the Linden Memorial Day Parade for the excellent community service he provided by hunting down returnable bottles, cleaning up the streets in the process. But as it turned out, things changed drastically for Eddie shortly after that article was published.

With his mother receiving full-time assistance, Eddie's care fell to his younger brother Rick, who soon placed Eddie in an adult foster care home about a half hour's drive from his mother and about an hour from me. By the time I learned Eddie was so close, he had been living there five years. My sister had sent him a cell phone, and since Eddie has always loved gadgets, I offered to take him headphones to go with it. When I called Eddie on the cell phone and told him I'd be there the next day, he sang, "Goody, goody," in his happy and faintly familiar tone, delighted to hear from me.

My sister called shortly after Eddie and I hung up. She'd been exchanging emails with Rick and had mentioned my plans to visit Eddie. Rick's response, strongly warning me against visiting his brother, hit her like a cannon ball. Rick emailed her a dirty laundry list of all the reasons I should stay away from Eddie and insisted it was for my own safety, explaining that his brother wasn't the same person we remembered. Based on his description, Eddie had become a thief, a beggar, and a liar who wandered the streets like a diabolical destitute.

Rick's email failed to hit its mark. Had he remembered anything about me, he would have known that such a bizarre warning would merely boost my resolve to visit Eddie, not scare me away. After all, I was the same the tomboy who hadn't cried when Rick's puck had smacked me in the throat during one of our neighborhood hockey games. I was the same defender of small amphibians who'd thrown rocks at him as he hurled toads at the concrete wall at the bridge. Nonetheless, I sensed that Rick felt judged for not doing enough for his brother and was letting this emotion interfere with what was best for Eddie.

"That's not the Eddie I remember, and I don't believe him," I responded.

Though my life was in a state of flux, I couldn't wait to see Eddie. Besides the fact that my husband and I had a daughter starting college, a son in high school, and a house full of pets, I was a partner in a residential building business with my brother-in-law, and things weren't going well. He had developed a practice of playing musical chairs with business partners who weren't always in tune with his ideas, and was unscrupulously conspiring to remove my chair as soon as the music stopped. I was ripe for distraction, so despite my busy schedule, the hour-long drive from my toxic work environment to see Eddie couldn't have come at a better time.

Something else propelled me, too. Though I didn't understand it at the time, it's now quite clear that visiting Eddie brought me back to the idyllic days we had spent together when we were young. In hindsight, I might have predicted that by the time I dropped off Eddie after our first visit, my focus had shifted from the genuine difficulties I was undergoing to being able to notice and appreciate the good things in my life, just like he always had. My visit left me genuinely concerned about Eddie's welfare, since he appeared to live in abject squalor, but little did I know how this brief initial visit would change life for both of us. What I did know was that our time together had immediately reminded me of how skilled Eddie was at allowing good things to happen. More than ever, I was ready to learn how he did it.

Like his favorite TV heroes—John Wayne, the Lone Ranger, Chuck Connors, Chuck Norris, and Elvis Presley, Eddie has always made the right move just in the nick of time. And from the beginning, Eddie Lee was forced to become adept at survival.

On an early summer morning in 1952, a woman from social services arrived at a small ramshackle house located in a modest Central Michigan town accompanied by a police officer. A nervous young couple opened the door, prepared for her arrival. The woman had been there before, and now she was returning, court order in hand, to take their two children into custody. Having fallen on hard times since the father lost his job, the couple didn't deny that their two scrubby tykes walked the streets, knocking on doors and begging for food. The couple understood that they couldn't care for their children and that giving custody to the state was the best and only thing to do.

Eddie's mother went to say goodbye to the children while the social worker gathered her things and explained the last details to Eddie's father. Just then, the mound of newspapers lying next to her on the couch began to stir. The social worker carefully peeled back the papers, expecting to find a burrowed cat or even a mouse. Instead, she uncovered the worst possible news buried beneath the day's headlines: a strikingly malnourished infant with a fresh rat bite on his nose and claw marks on his face.

The woman gasped in disbelief at the sight of the starving infant who had somehow mustered the strength to rustle the papers. She stood up and scowled at the couple, gathered the two older kids, and exited through the front door, shouting her plans to return for the baby as the door banged behind her. Sure enough, she returned the next morning. Just like they had for his heroes, the right things happened at the right time for Eddie.

Adopting a child with an intellectual disability was as unusual in 1952 as it is today and was particularly uncommon in rural counties in the middle of Michigan. There weren't many couples looking for babies at all, much less babies with special needs, but one couple took their doctor's advice and stopped by the adoption agency since they were having trouble conceiving. They were told a few children under five were available for adoption as well as a baby who might have some mental retardation caused by malnourishment.

The moment Tilly walked past Eddie at the adoption agency, something sparked. The baby's eyes locked on her, and that was that. Tilly was smitten. She knew she had found her baby, or maybe he had found her. "There was just something about the way that little baby looked at me," she told her relatives. "The second I saw him, I told Allen, 'He needs us as much as we need him.'"

According to Tilly, at three months, Eddie was still so small that he fit into a milk bottle. In addition to being developmentally delayed and legally blind in one eye, his starvation had caused permanent brain damage, but Tilly didn't care. She didn't consult any doctors or specialists seeking the probability of Eddie's condition improving, nor did she investigate the severity of his brain injury. She simply accepted him for who he was.

Tilly and Allen Lee decided to take Eddie home. More accurately, Tilly made the decision. After the adoption process was complete, she sent Allen back to the agency to button up the details and bring the baby home while she finished last-minute preparations. She didn't realize Allen was still unsure about the whole idea. As soon as he walked into the house without Eddie, she turned him around and sent him back to get her baby. Tilly was sharply intelligent and possessed a quick wit, qualities that weren't noteworthy or appreciated in women of her time. She also was wise enough not to let the opinions and judgments of others interfere with her decisions. As she often said, she didn't listen to any of that malarkey. She had decided to raise Eddie as her own, and that's exactly what she did. What's more, despite her doctor's initial assessment that she might not be able to conceive a child, she and Allen went on to become the biological parents of Eddie's younger brother Rick.

From the beginning, Eddie's mother knew her adopted son's physical and mental development would be significantly boosted by exercise, just like other children. Indeed, Eddie's most striking developmental challenges were his small size—at twelve months, he was still bottle-fed, since solid food was difficult for him to digest—and his slow motor skills. His vision was also compromised and would go on to deteriorate even further in his adult life, but for now, Tilly knew just what he needed—a bike.

As soon as he could walk, Eddie's mother placed him on the brand new tricycle. She coaxed him with a little push, helping him steer, but he couldn't keep his tiny feet on the pedals. She worked with him as he attempted to get the rhythm down, keeping his little fingers gripping the handlebars with one hand while holding his feet to the pedals through each completed circular motion with the other. When she realized that function was a bigger deal than form, she tied his feet to the pedals with shoestrings. Before long, Eddie was riding his trike like they were molded together.

Turns out, Tilly was incredibly wise; throughout his life, Eddie's ability to ride a bike has been the basis of his social interactions and very likely his physical health.

I met Eddie and Rick soon after my family moved in down the street from them. I was eight, and Eddie was fifteen. Shortly after our arrival, Eddie welcomed us to the neighborhood with a fistful of feathers from the peacocks his father kept in pens behind their house. It was clear right away that Eddie actively recruited new friends whenever the opportunity arose. With seven Keating kids right down the street, he'd hit the jackpot. The Lee boys instantly became part of our family, with Eddie regularly stopping by on his bike. That bike was an expression of his self-image as the ultimate good guy, the action hero. Sometimes he pretended it was a motor-cycle, revving the engine; at other times he became a cowboy and the bike was his horse.

When other kids made fun of him for his disability, which they frequently did, Eddie found freedom and companionship on his bike; but no teasing, ridiculing, or badgering could bother Eddie for long. We were amazed at how quickly he recovered from hurt feelings. He'd ride his bike over to tell us what some ignorant kid had said or done, and as soon as we offered to kick that punk out of the county, Eddie was as good as new. He'd go right on to the next thing, whether it was demonstrating the sign language he'd just learned at the special education school he referred to as "workshop" or reporting how many suckers he'd caught fishing down at the bridge. There were plenty of times when he plopped himself down on our front porch, head hang-ing, waiting for one of us to come out and console him, but he didn't come over to keep the hurt going. He considered us master electri-cians when it came to flipping on his happy switch.

When we were kids, I honestly thought I was only helping Eddie by being his friend. Today, I know I simply wasn't as wise as he was. Being there for him also helped me. By providing Eddie the support he needed, he made me see how insignificant my problems were.

What's more, he helped me see that laughing at them immediately made them shrink to a much more manageable size.

Since those first years when we laughed about bullies on the porch, Eddie has always been on the move. As a teenager, he was happiest when doing something—either riding his bike, walking, or stopping in at the grocery store where his mother worked in the meat department. Whenever he was doing something, he ended up meeting people, and every time he met people, he ended up with a job. If we didn't see him for a few days, it was a sure bet he had found someone who needed his help.

One night, Eddie stopped by sporting a couple of long, nasty scratches on his arms. I asked him what had happened, expecting to hear about a bike mishap, but he explained that he'd been rounding up turkeys to be loaded on trucks at a farm down the road. His scarred up arms were a pretty good indication that turkeys put up quite a fight when it came time to load them and it wasn't easy to outsmart them. Eddie quickly got the hang of his new job and soon became that farm's most skilled and dependable turkey rustler.

Some of Eddie's jobs were part-time, some were seasonal, some lasted a day or two, and many simply consisted of giving someone a quick hand. The duration of the job or the amount of money he earned didn't matter to Eddie. What counted was feeling valued and appreciated. Thinking about Eddie's genuine enjoyment of every job, whether great or small, makes me suspect that many of us emphasize how much time we spend working either to satisfy a resume or to puff ourselves up, especially when statistics show that most people don't really enjoy the hours they spend doing what they're paid to do. It might do us some good to forget about the paycheck for a minute and instead simply appreciate the service we provide to the people we work with every day. After all, the paycheck reflects the balance we agreed to receive, while the amount of service we are willing to provide shows how much we value ourselves and others.

Eddie truly does value people. Facebook founder Mark Zuckerberg could have modeled his social media platform around Eddie's approach. Eddie's network empire has been built face to face, both on foot and with the use of his bike. If someone is nice to him, they are added to Eddie's network, and this is as true today as it was when we were young.

As kids, we spent the majority of our summer days swimming at the bridge. There, Eddie helped us come out of our shells. The bridge was only a short bike ride from our house, down a dirt road, and it was our favorite neighborhood hangout. Since we couldn't fathom sharing it with strangers, we always asked Eddie to ride ahead to see if the coast was clear. He would valiantly take off with his jaw thrust forward, aviator sunglasses in place and a towel wrapped around his neck, a cross between Elvis and Paul Revere, anxious to report back. If someone was at the bridge, he'd come back and tell us he knew them—which often meant he had just met them a minute ago—and we'd all be coaxed into going. This networking passion has stuck with Eddie throughout his life. Wherever he has lived, he has connected people to people, making them all feel included.

Of course, as well as being a symbol of his independence, Eddie's bike has played a huge role in his ability to connect with others. When Allen died, Tilly's health was poor, so she initially went to live with Rick and his family. When Rick didn't invite Eddie to come along, Eddie had his first experience living in the adult foster care system. Since his bike wasn't sent with him, Eddie was shut off from the world. After learning about several degrading experiences Eddie endured in care homes, Tilly bought a home in the community of Linden so she and Eddie could live together again. Complete with a new bike, Eddie was once again free, and he soon spread himself out doing what he did best: finding and turning in bottles and cans and collecting friends along the way.

After an injury, Tilly was forced to move into a nursing home in a nearby community. The house had to be sold, and Eddie was once again displaced. He lived alone in an apartment over a local bar for a short period, adding visits to Tilly to his daily rounds on his bike. Since his monthly social security checks didn't quite cover the rent, he went to work sweeping the floors at the barbershop and walking dogs. In spite of his efforts, his expenses soon became too much. Friends took him in as they could, hoping a less expensive living arrangement would surface, but when it didn't, his brother found the adult foster care home for him in Highland, Michigan. This time, Eddie had his bike, or at least at first he did.

By the time Eddie went to Highland, he was developing cataracts, which further compromised his diminished eyesight. This made it more challenging to find bottles and also made it much more dangerous, since he was riding along busier roads. Instead of working with Rick to arrange the surgery he needed, Eddie's caregiver at the home took his bike away, without considering how much this would affect Eddie's wellbeing. Eddie didn't understand why, but he was certain that he was being punished.

During my first visit, at Eddie's urging, we walked behind the shed that sat behind the driveway to check on his bike. There it was, leaning on the outside of the structure, along with a dirty, donated bike trailer he had used for hauling bottles and cans. Now, since he couldn't ride, Eddie had taken to walking up and down the road, combing the area for bottles and collecting them in garbage bags he'd brought along. He also walked to church and accepted rides from people he met there. Nothing could ebb Eddie's desire live his life fully, not even losing his bike and his eyesight.

This active lifestyle has kept Eddie physically and emotionally healthy throughout his life. He's so involved with walking, volunteering, visiting friends, and working that there isn't much time to squeeze in many sniffles.

Today, many years after we first met, Eddie's habit of spending much of his day on his bike remains unchanged. He calls me often to report that he's out riding with his friends from BrickWays, the non-profit organization in Traverse City, Michigan, that helps adults with developmental disabilities live independently in the community. Other times, Eddie fills me in about his productive day at work, bottle picking, or just goofing around feeling happy. He'll ask me when I'm heading north so we can ride our bikes together. After all, there are always new things to show me. Eddie focuses on feeling good and being happy—and that makes for a very effective and affordable health care plan.

Nearly all health experts agree on the many benefits of incorporating exercise into a daily routine. At the same time, being out in the community at any level connects us with opportunities we wouldn't otherwise experience. Staying active physically and socially is the perfect recipe for keeping our bodies and souls in tune. The most important ingredient in this recipe is doing what makes us feel good, because this puts us in a prime position to think more clearly and forgive more freely. Spending time with others, especially people we care about, offers many of the same advantages. Being socially active allows us to share what makes us unique and at the same time reveals how much we have in common.

Eddie combines exercise and socializing effortlessly. Experts say it takes ten thousand hours of practice to master a skill, but Eddie's accomplishments can be measured in miles. He logs over five thousand miles a year on his bike just riding around town. This no doubt qualifies him as an overachiever, but because biking is tied to his social life, it never feels like work. Whenever the urge strikes, Eddie hops on his red ten-speed and starts riding up and down the streets, attracting a following like he's behind the wheel of a Good Humor truck.

More than sixty years after Tilly tied his tiny feet to the tricycle pedals, Eddie still likes to start every day with a bike ride. He knows there's always someone or something new out there to appreciate. For Eddie, nothing is more fun than hopping on his hot rod and going out to find it.

BELIEVE IN YOURSELF

"Believe in yourself, and there will come a day when others will have no choice but to believe in you."

—CYNTHIA KERSEY

Whether you are proficient at riding a bike, a camel, or a wave, chances are you didn't master it the first time you tried. It took some getting used to, and practice undoubtedly helped you gain confidence in your ability to reach your goals. The more we devote ourselves to what we want to master, the better we get at it. This is why so many sports teams practice just as hard in the off-season as they do when it counts.

It also helps to have some coaching and encouragement from people around you who remind you that they have your back. Even with all the help from the sidelines, there always seem to be people who have a hard time believing we're good enough to suit up at game time. They dish out their reasons, fortified with worst-case scenarios, to explain why we shouldn't get too serious about meeting our goals.

On some level, these well-meaning people are helpful, because what they're really asking is how bad you want to win. Eddie has taught me that you win every time you accept such opinions gracefully, dispose of them quietly, and then go out and practice. Indeed, growing up down the road from Eddie helped me debunk many of the limiting beliefs about the world that I was beginning to absorb—especially the belief that our capacity for success is defined by our book smarts. The day I met Eddie, that logic began to crumble. Eddie was constantly creating something new to learn or do or be. With the courageous help of his mother, whose encouragement was as magical as a bowl of Lucky Charms, he gracefully leaped over any doubts about his abilities that might have been formed by the opinions of others.

The summer after we moved into our new house just outside of Carson City, our grandparents came from their home in Detroit to stay with us. A couple of days after they arrived, Grandpa volunteered to take us swimming at Crystal Lake, a small vacation spot about eight miles northwest of us. Since we didn't go there often, we relished the opportunity and immediately scrambled to find our swimsuits. This presented a bit of a challenge, since we normally swam at the bridge down the road wearing the driest cutoffs and t-shirts we could find.

We had just gathered up our towels and were waiting for Grandpa when Eddie stopped by. As usual, he showed up right on time. When we asked if he wanted to come along, he boomeranged home and back dressed in his swimming trunks faster than he could let out a howl. Then we piled into Grandpa's black Chevy Impala and took off, fueled with enough enthusiasm to rocket us to the moon.

Grandpa's car was packed full of Keating kids ranging in age from five to ten along with our eight-year-old aunt plus sixteen-year-old Eddie. Crystal Lake, which was semitransparent at best, had a nice public sandy beach situated directly across the street from a Dairy Queen. Next to that was the Lakeside Bar and Grill, a popular restaurant that offered live entertainment on weekends and food and spirits all the time. Its proximity to the lake made it the perfect indoor adult break room.

As soon as we arrived at the beach, Grandpa took us across the street and bought us cotton candy three times the size of our heads along with giant sticks of saltwater taffy that stuck to the roofs of our mouths, creating temporary communication challenges on top of facial distortions. We pried the candy out with our fingertips and hurried back across the street, making a beeline for the water like sugar donuts headed for a dunk in a glass of milk, eager to leap in and dissolve our sticky candy coating.

"Whoa!" Grandpa called, holding up his large hand like an undercover scout leader. "When I raise my hand like this, you need to come out of the water and wait here so I can go across the street for a drink."

Grandpa calmly raised his hand above his head, demonstrating the signal. He called out a reminder not to drink the lake water—you never knew what the other kids were doing in it—and off we went, headed for the warm water packed with kids tossing beach balls, flipping their fins, and playing periscope with plastic snorkels.

After about twenty minutes, a mere blink of an eye, we saw the first hand signal. My brother called us and we obediently filed onto the beach, sitting in Grandpa's spot as he ambled across the street and disappeared into the Lakeside. We knew Grandpa liked to have a drink, and we decided this was only fair, since he was dedicating the entire afternoon to our pursuit of fun. We kept our eyes fixed on the door that faced south, squealing with delight when we saw him emerge from the bar. As he crossed the street, Grandpa gave us the all-clear signal and we bolted back into the water, splashing about like freshly snagged fish. It seemed like we had just acclimated ourselves to the water temperature again when his giant hand rose above the horizon. Grudgingly, we exited the water, sensing a pattern we didn't like. Without a word, Grandpa turned and headed along the trail he was personally blazing to the Lakeside. Sometime later, the all-clear signal had us once again charging for the water.

The third time Grandpa's hand went up, we emerged onto the beach dripping with anguish as he sauntered across the street to quench his thirst. We could have filled the impressions our wet bathing suit bottoms made in the sand with enough tears to create our own private swimming holes. We focused on feeling sorry for ourselves as if we'd never feel the rippled sand under the somewhat clear water again. Our agony turned minutes of waiting into illusionary hours.

Tellingly, the exception to this sob story was Eddie. Each time we were called out of the water, Eddie saw an opportunity to explore the beach. He proceeded to walk along the shore, mingle with other sunbathers, and thoroughly enjoy himself. I watched in annoyance as he sashayed across the sand, reminding everyone he met what a perfectly beautiful day it was, striking up bubbly conversations, accepting snacks, and collecting small treasures that had been left behind. I recall wondering how he could be happy at the exact moment we were being denied the fun we'd been promised. It didn't dawn on me that Eddie had the right idea—so many other opportunities for fun were right there in front of us. Instead of sitting there complaining in my soggy swimsuit, I could have been building sandcastles, collecting skeletons of water critters, or just laughing at the funny antics going on around me.

I watched Eddie turn and make his way back towards us. When he saw us in the same place—or, perhaps, in the same state of mind—his radar guided him to swivel in the other direction, seeking a more affable atmosphere. Unlike Grandpa and the rest of us, who thought we needed to be drinking in the Lakeside or swimming in the lake to be happy, Eddie knew that swimming was but one item on an endless list of ways to have fun. What's more, he didn't need anyone but himself to accomplish it. With his spout always open, his glass was undeniably half full.

Once again, Grandpa walked out the door of the bar and wobbled back across the street toward the beach. As soon as he arrived on our side of the street, we bolted for the water as if it were an oasis in the middle of the desert. Before we could reach it, he signaled for us to stop and said, "It's time to go home, kids." We listened warily to his announcement and then reluctantly began gathering our wet towels. Though we cleaned our feet the best we could, we still managed to change the interior of the Impala from black to sand as we squeezed ourselves into the car in the same order we'd arrived in. Eddie sat next to Grandpa in the front with my oldest brother Keith on the passenger side as Grandpa pulled out of the parking lot and drove away from Crystal Lake.

As soon as we left the lake that late afternoon, Grandpa realized he was one hundred percent intoxicated. He turned onto the first dirt road he could find outside the city limits. Flanked by open fields and lined with occasional trees, the road was clear of traffic as far as we could see. For a few minutes, Grandpa drove slowly down the road, kicking up dust, and then he stopped, realizing he couldn't safely drive in his current state no matter how careful he was.

"I need someone to drive," he announced, gazing into the rearview mirror and then to his right. He focused on Eddie as soberly as he could. "Eddie, can you drive?" "Yes, I can," Eddie replied, thrusting his jaw outward in a display of supreme confidence. We looked at Grandpa for a sign that he wasn't serious, and when it dawned on us that he was, we parted our blue lips in unison and blurted out a shrill and unified "No!"

Without hesitation, we elected Keith to be the designated driver, but Grandpa slurred that Keith was too young. "No, Keith can drive! He's been driving his whole life!" we pleaded, although Keith was only ten years old and couldn't reach the pedals. Grandpa insisted that Eddie would drive us home, so Eddie struggled out of his seat and stumbled around the front of the car, bouncing off the bumper as he felt his way to the driver's side and slid behind the wheel. When he was ready to shift into drive, he squeezed his hands together in a tight ball while clenching his jaw, a gesture he often displayed when he was excited. We weren't sure if Grandpa knew about Eddie's intellectual disability, and we didn't want to say any-thing that would hurt our friend's feelings, especially since he was sitting in the driver's seat, so off we went. Nonetheless, we honed our back-seat driving skills all the way home, gawking like chickens loaded up for slaughter. Through it all, Eddie kept his eyes and his attention on the road, thoroughly tuning us out.

Thanks to our differently-abled and highly capable neighbor, we made it home safely, despite our verbal interference. Once we arrived, we quietly scattered without saying a word to our parents. We were particularly careful to not mention anything to our grandmother, who no doubt would have pulled the plug on Grandpa driving us anywhere ever again. Swimming at Crystal Lake was too dear to give up regardless of the mode of transportation it took to get there.

On a Sunday morning soon after, we watched from our front yard as Mrs. Lees' sedan drove by with Eddie behind the wheel. Tooting the horn and waving to us, he happily drove his mother to church. We looked at each other in disbelief. Eddie did know how to drive! How had we not noticed this before?

Despite Grandpa's clouded judgment that day, he had seen something in Eddie that we hadn't—the unflinching allegiance of a member of the royal guard. Eddie's display of self-confidence was so strong that Grandpa knew we were in far more capable hands with Eddie behind the wheel than with him. As for Eddie, he'd already learned to filter the opinions of others properly—in one ear and out the other—without letting them influence his ability to perform yet always remaining mindful of his capabilities. His mother had nurtured him by omitting the lessons many dutiful parents teach their children, the ones that encourage proceeding with extreme caution before trying anything that isn't a sure bet. Tilly hadn't offered Eddie any special treatment or coddling growing up. Instead, she'd provided him with an invaluable education by coaching him to keep stretching himself and trying new experiences, something most people shy away from. Eddie's job was to believe in himself wholeheartedly. He did this so well that he sometimes surprised himself with what he could do. As a fringe benefit, he often shocked others, too.

Looking back, it would have been easy for Eddie to live on the sidelines. This could have happened had he listened to the skepticism that came from well-meaning friends. He would have been still worse off had he listened to the opinions of the not-so-well-intended nincompoops he has crossed throughout his life, yet Eddie's self-worth is on par with the net worth of a corporate CEO. His talents are born and bred through his imagination. Instead of wishing he could do something, he sets his sights on what he wants to learn and studies the successful tricks, moves, and techniques of his favorite idols. Then he steps into the shoes of the professional he aims to be by acting the part, even printing business cards to prove it. There is no doubt in

Eddie's mind that he's the real deal when he pulls out a business card that touts his title and proudly puts it in the hands of a new contact. Even so, when he offers up his services, it isn't about the money. Eddie's reward is the act of sharing his talents with anyone who is open to a warm greeting or needs a helping hand.

It can feel disheartening when others lack faith in our abilities, especially when we're so certain we can pull something off that we can taste it. It's even worse when those negative opinions come from the very people whose support we thought we could count on. But that doesn't mean we have to throw in the towel. Just like Eddie that warm summer day decades ago, we are in the driver's seat. It may be helpful to consider that anyone else's opinion about the cusccess of our goals is merely a reflection on whether they think they could accomplish it. As long as there is a dream worth pursuing there will be some push-back. Henry Ford was no stranger to naysayers; many of them were his own employees. He silenced many skeptics when he candidly remarked, "Whether you think you can or whether you think you can't, you're right."

Upon being forced to alter our limiting beliefs about Eddie's aptitude, we Keating kids learned just as much about his character. Eddie was so confident in his driving ability that he shrugged off our skepticism, ignored our rants, and proceeded to steer Grandpa's Impala with the skill of a licensed driver, even though our protests shook the car as if Elvis Presley himself were gyrating in the back.

Letting it roll off his back like Eddie does takes some effort. Without Tilly's encouragement, he probably couldn't have done it as easily. This is precisely why it's so important to offer our support to others. When we set aside our beliefs and judgments about what we think is possible, offering encouragement instead of criticism to those who want to try something new, we unveil our own untapped potential, too. Applying this lesson helps us change our opinions about what we or anyone else should or shouldn't do. Then, instead of judging them, we can offer our full support. Giving someone a motivational push is always appreciated, and as soon as we let go of their handlebars, we set them free.

The truth is, we humans are immensely powerful beings. We arrive on Earth equipped with all the knowhow we need to succeed, as long we are curious, interested, and persistent enough to keep moving toward our goals. All the gizmos we utilize every day exist because someone didn't stop believing in the ideas behind them, regardless of the opinions of others or the lack of college degrees often perceived to be the only route to success. All successful people have at least one thing in common: when they were at the bottom rung of the proverbial ladder, they had the right amount of encouragement from someone who believed in them and their crazy dreams. This encouragement helped them stay focused on their goals and drowned out the grumbling naysayers.

The Eddie Lee I know today isn't so different from the teenager who safely drove our bathing suit-clad family home all those years ago. Decades later, Eddie is still the same confident boy who got behind the wheel of our grandfather's Impala. When he decides he wants to learn a new skill, he tackles it with confidence. He employs his positive attitude wherever he goes, applies a practiced focus, and acts the part. I always know he's hot on the trail of success when he calls to request new business cards.

For Eddie, seeing the new title under his name is the icing on the cake, and that makes it a done deal. Unlike many people who let their fear of failure get in the way of their desires, he makes a decision and then focuses on it like a laser beam. When it comes to making it real, Eddie uses his imagination and plays his part to the hilt.

There's a lot to be said for practical experience, the kind you don't find in a classroom, and there are many ways to further your education beyond traditional sources. Despite our screams of terror that long-ago summer day, Eddie convinced us there was no one more competent or cooler under pressure. He believed in himself. In so doing, he showed us how to do the same.

KNOW YOU WILL BE OKAY

"Life isn't about waiting for the storm to pass;
it's about learning how to dance in the rain."

—VIVIAN GREENE

None of us touch down on this planet excited about the prospect of experiencing fear or suffering, much less the need to fight for survival; we would much rather experience a made-for-television version of someone else's survival story from the safety of our sofas. Survival in real life is a test of will, patience, and grace that often requires keeping quiet and cooperating with our aggressors. Although we always want to express ourselves freely with the radio frequency tuned to the music of our muse, it isn't always that simple.

Despite our best intentions to steer clear of danger, many of us encounter terrible atrocities and hardships at the hands of individuals who don't feel good about themselves. At their own peril, these individuals misuse their power, taking their frustrations out on whoever is available. They can target anyone, but more times than not, the victims are people in need of regular assistance and care—in many ways the most innocent, trusting, and vulnerable among us.

Luckily, we are born armed with intuition. We can use this intuition not only to step in when something doesn't feel right, helping to spot abuse and rescue victims, but also when we ourselves are the victims. Our inherent skills and impulses help us come to our own aid when we're in dangerous or uncomfortable circumstances out of our control, and this is as true for Eddie as it is for anyone.

Eddie knows he can rely on his instincts. Just like the Lone Ranger never saddles up without Tonto, Eddie's intuition rides alongside him like a trusted best friend. Based on how he has transformed his times of turbulence into triumph, it's easy to see that Eddie decided early on not to live in a state of hopelessness or victimhood. He chooses to see something good in every circumstance, and since he is the commander in chief of his own air traffic control system, he takes responsibility for keeping his runway cleared for happy landings. Eddie has endured his share of hard times and could easily have used them as an excuse to gain sympathy from others, but hard luck stories don't interest him unless the good guy grins in the end.

Eddie's first survival maneuver came right at the beginning of his life. From beneath the debris on the couch where he lay hidden, he did the only thing he knew to do to get help: he moved. He didn't do it to get back at his parents for starving him under their care; presumably they were doing the best they could. His call to action came in the form of a nudge from deep inside his soul, and with the slight rustle of the newspapers and the help of an observant saint of a social worker, he set the wheels in motion to begin solving every problem he had. His parents were spared further guilt and anguish over their inability to provide basic care for their infant, and Eddie was free to explore the big world that awaited him. He could have lived the rest of what would have been a very short life undiscovered, quiet as a church mouse, but his survival instinct kicked in. This was not his time to cash in his chips, and somehow he knew it.

Eddie went into safe mode at other times during his childhood. It turned out that Allen lacked Tilly's patience and understanding, and sometimes he took it out on Eddie and Rick. We witnessed a few marked events as kids walking by their house, and more than once we saw looks of fear on their faces when their father yelled at them. Since we considered the Lee boys part of our family, it was difficult to see them hurt or afraid, but Eddie survived it all. Even when he had opportunities to complain about the way he was being treated, he instinctively chose to cross over to the sunny side of the street rather than engage us in his dilemma. He clearly didn't want to spend time seeing the world through the eyes of a victim.

Eddie went on to be mistreated again in life. When I made my first trip to visit him at the adult foster care home in Highland, I didn't know what to expect. I'd heard stories about the lack of regulation and scrutiny many of these facilities operate under, leaving them ripe for dishonest and deceitful caregivers who provide marginal care, and my presumption was underpinned by reading Rick's email to my sister wherein he admitted the place was a "dump." Painting Eddie as a derelict and misfit who couldn't be placed in homes that provided better accommodations because he was such a troublemaker, Rick claimed that Eddie had to go there because no one else would take him.

In spite of my misgivings, I wasn't prepared for the sense of hopelessness I felt when I pulled into the driveway and found Eddie standing near the fallout shelter of the decrepit farmhouse he now called home. This building was a far cry from the neatly maintained red ranch he had lived in growing up filled with beautifully chiming grandfather clocks his father had collected. As I looked at Eddie for the first time in years, I contemplated the warnings I'd heard. It was comforting to see, just as I'd imagined, that Eddie was no monster. He was the same kindhearted individual, inside and out, who had grown up down the street from me. All that had changed were his age and his living conditions, and the latter appeared to have been downgraded to deplorable.

I stayed as long as I could that first day, and though Eddie invited me to come inside, I didn't feel comfortable enough to enter. Before I left, I asked how he was being treated. He indicated that everything was okay and changed the subject by introducing me to his roommate, Noelle, who had just come outside and stood quietly next to him. Eddie made a point of sharing that Noelle became his friend and comrade the day he moved in, and he nodded with approval when Noelle agreed. As I backed out of the driveway and waved to the two of them, Eddie and Noelle stood as still as statues, watching me.

Driving away, I felt distinctly ill at ease. I was returning to a safe home in a pleasant suburb while my childhood neighbor was standing in a muddy unkempt driveway, waiting, at least in my imagination, for my return. After just one visit, I felt incredibly responsible for Eddie's welfare. I knew I couldn't ignore the fact that he seemed to need someone to step in and help.

Signs that Eddie was being mistreated appeared almost immediately. Eddie had a cell phone that my sister had sent him because it was so difficult to reach him on the house's phone line. As long as I'd known him, Eddie had spent the better part of his days outdoors, so this part made sense. The problem was, a few days after I reconnected with him, I received a disturbing call from Rick. Reminiscent of the calls he'd made to my sister, he portrayed Eddie as nothing but a criminal and street walker. After that, every call I made to Eddie went directly to voicemail.

Worried about his safety, I called the house line continuously, determined to find out if he was okay. Finally, the daughter of Eddie's caregiver answered and summoned Eddie to the phone. When I asked where his cell phone was, Eddie dodged the question, so I told him I was coming to see him the following day. When I got there, he admitted his caregiver had taken his phone away. It was obvious that Eddie's ability to communicate with people who could help him was being stifled. Just as concerning was the fact that he'd been led to believe he was doing something wrong and was being punished for it.

My greatest challenge in getting involved with Eddie's care had nothing to do with him and everything to do with me. I felt overwhelmed even without Eddie in my life, and I was unsure of what I could do to help him. I was used to breaking projects down by line item and order of importance, but there was so much Eddie needed that it was difficult to know where to begin. I decided to start with safety and began asking him questions about his care and treatment as we drove to stores and errands, bringing the topic up casually so as not to put him on the spot. As with the cell phone, he dodged my questions like he was skiing on a slalom course. He responded to every query that made him uncomfortable by looking the other way, commenting on something to divert my attention, or, if we were walking, by suddenly losing his balance and verbally correcting himself. These were the same techniques I recalled him using when we were young whenever a subject made him uncomfortable. I took his cue and decided to let things surface at his initiation.

In retrospect, I came to understand that Eddie was teaching me that I didn't need to take control or grasp every nuance of what he was experiencing. Eventually, I started to see that despite my idea of how things appeared, Eddie was making choices that were right for him, something he had been doing for a long time. He had become a master at keeping his sights on doing the things that mattered and that pleased him, no matter how crappy the situation appeared. I decided my role for now was to pay attention, and if and when Eddie needed me to intervene, I would do so.

Not long after this epiphany, something did surface, but instead of coming from Eddie, it came from his caregiver. One afternoon while I was dropping Eddie off with his groceries, the caregiver met me in the driveway. While Eddie was busy taking bags into the house, the caregiver asked if Eddie had reported being choked, shoved, or locked in the cellar.

I replied honestly that Eddie had never mentioned any physical mistreatment. In response, the caregiver began assuring me that Eddie had a habit of telling cockamamie stories of abuse to anyone who would listen, but since he was treated so well in their home, I shouldn't believe any of it.

This was the second time I had been told, without solicitation, that Eddie wasn't credible and that everything he said was nonsense.

It was true that Eddie hadn't said anything to me about being locked in the cellar or mistreated physically at this facility. He had described being punched, slapped, and scratched in other homes but had been mum about this one, other than sharing occasional painful feelings about verbal swipes that had wounded him as deeply as any punch ever could. I had always known Eddie to be honest, and after listening to his caregiver, I was more concerned about what Eddie wasn't saying than about what he was. It made sense that he was open about his past experiences with abuse given that he couldn't be harmed by anyone from those places anymore. They were in his past, so he felt safe talking about them. This situation was different.

After we moved Eddie out of the foster home and into ours, we decided to take some action against the caregiver to prevent further harm to others that were living under their care in the same unde-sirable conditions. My husband had reported the abuses and unjust practices of the facility to adult protective services under the depart-ment of human services, and within a month the home was closed down. It was clear that the caregiver knew how to work the system, because he immediately hop-scotched his way to the county directly north of him and opened up a new group home.

This isn't an uncommon practice in the adult care industry. It's easy for places like these to stay in business, since they can move their clients right along with them. Many people under the care of such facilities don't have anyone to advocate for them, and some have families that have already decided this is the best they can do for their loved ones, which explains why some homes get away with serial abuses for a long time.

It turned out that for the duration of Eddie's time at the home, every one of his social security checks had gone directly from Eddie's brother Rick, who acted as the representative payee, to the caregiver without a dime of money going to Eddie. Reading through the con-ditions of care, we learned that Eddie should have received a small stipend from every check. Over the years, this added up to quite a sum, so we decided to ask the court to award Eddie some of the money that had been withheld.

When Dennis took Eddie to the courtroom to testify, Eddie took one look at his brother and former caregiver and froze. He had been so programmed to fear what they could do to him that he couldn't think. When the judge asked Eddie what he was there for, he responded sheepishly that he didn't know. Instead of attempting to understand the circumstances and act with sensitivity to Eddie's developmen-tal disabilities, the judge chose the path of least resistance, assuring himself an early lunch to boot. He claimed he couldn't make a ruling on Eddie's case since it involved federal money.

Sensing from the judge's comments that he wouldn't support Eddie's request, Rick smugly attempted to close the case by converting the courtroom into a circus funhouse complete with smoke and mirrors. Without flinching, he described the adult foster care home as a wonderful place and the caregiver as a kind and thoughtful provider for Eddie's special needs.

At this point, Dennis had heard enough. "Really?" he asked Rick and the caregiver. "It's so nice that the Department of Health and Human Services came in and closed you down, correct?"

As the two men looked at him in disbelief, Dennis confirmed, "That's right, I'm the one who placed the call. They couldn't believe the pathetic conditions you had these people living in."

Those who suffer physical or emotional abuse have to decide how and when to reach out for help. In Eddie's case, this meant keeping quiet and putting up with it until he was ready, with assistance, to take action. Although he needs help making decisions and handling finances and paperwork, Eddie is his own legal guardian, something his parents saw to long ago at the advice of their attorney. Even though he didn't choose to live in this abusive facility, in the end the choice to stay or leave was his.

The best thing we could do was bring Eddie the help he needed to climb out of the hole and onto firm ground. On his own terms, Eddie made the decision to move. Having done so, he felt no need to revisit the past or get even with anybody in order to, as he says, "Get outta Dodge." We simply needed to get out of his way and let him take the lead.

It took awhile for Eddie to open up about the seven years he lived in that care home. He remembers holidays being the loneliest, especially Christmas. Without a way to spend the day with his mother at the nursing home, Christmas was a day to get through, not to celebrate. He and other care residents soberly watched the caregiver and his family exchange gifts while they expected and received nothing. Now, he shrugs off those times and names the people in the area that offered him friendship and support. Every now and then when memories of the foster home surface, he shrugs and says, "I'm glad I'm not mad anymore. My life is so much better."

Thanks to Eddie, I've come to believe that, regardless of what others say, there is nothing wrong with the decisions abused individuals make. In many cases, victims feel safer letting the situation play out than reaching out for help. Eddie knew that whenever he said something to others, his caregiver found ways to cut off his communication with them, so although it was difficult to watch and wait, we did things in Eddie's time. If anything, these experiences sharpened his intuition, since he learned to sense when it was best to stay silent. As for me, Eddie showed me that the best way to help him was to offer support and stay aware of what I observed, not try to take control.

Through it all, whenever he's needed it the most, Eddie's positive attitude has come to his rescue. To some people, his avoidance to speak up might be difficult to understand, but Eddie knows what works for him. He has no regrets about his decisions; he knows the best choice is always to follow his heart and listen to his instincts.

Once again, he was right—in his own way, in his own time, Eddie got himself out of the abusive living situation in Highland. Now, safely ensconced in the nurturing and stimulating environment he intends to remain in the rest of his life, he can enjoy watching cop shows and survival stories from the comfort of his couch, since he knows the good guys always come out on top in the end.

NEVER QUIT

"If you're interested, you will do what is most convenient;
if you're committed, you'll do whatever it takes."

—John Assaraf

Very few days go by without us making some kind of promise to do something or be somewhere for ourselves or someone else. Most of the commitments we agree to are a cinch and we follow through without a second thought, but others make us feel uncomfortable and require serious consideration. When deeper commitments make us genuinely nervous, we often respond in a way that makes us sound interested without promising anything more; that's when we come up with quasi-commitments like *Maybe, I'll try, I think so,* or *Let me check with the boss* instead of responding with an outright yes. Afterwards, avoiding following through on commitments we've made might seem like the best way to handle discomfort, but ask anyone who's been left at the altar, and they'll tell you it's a total copout. The truth is, when we shy away from keeping commitments we've made, we also miss out on the prospect of a miraculous transformation in personal growth, not to mention wedding cake.

No matter its size, every commitment we make and pledge to follow through with is tantamount to adding Miracle-Gro to a watering can before heading out to the garden. Simply put, the probability for success grows faster and stronger when we decide to follow through. Scientifically speaking, we fire up a whole new brain circuitry that helps us find ways to make our commitments come to life once we set the intention in motion. As a bonus, when we help others, we help ourselves. Many of us are stopped in our tracks by change because it challenges us to question our beliefs, but the growth we experience can take us places we never thought were possible.

Why is change so hard? According to "Abraham," a group consciousness from the non-physical dimension that is interpreted by Esther Hicks, it takes 17 seconds to manifest something new. That's it. But wait—there's more. Tack on another 30 days for us to talk ourselves into believing we can. For those of us who still resist our inner voice nudging us to jump in with both feet, it takes even longer; and sometimes changing a belief comes in a more jarring way—through a break up, a heart attack, a brush with the law, a near death experience, or a host of other ways we choose to receive our wake up call.

Of course, commitment begets commitment. When you purchase a car, you commit to the price, the cost of insurance, oil changes, new tires, and replacing every drop of gas it will burn. These are things few of us think about when we drive away enveloped in that new car smell. In the same way, having a baby is the beginning of a lifelong commitment to provide unconditional love, care, and support to another human being. It starts with conception and birth, but then we have to keep going. Our commitments bring out both our best intentions and our biggest resistance. Most of the time, we really don't have a full grasp on what we're getting into when we commit—or perhaps we refuse to let the details derail us from following through with our decisions.

The most endearing and rewarding of all commitments are those that come straight from the heart without the expectation of anything in return. These commitments define us. When Tilly adopted Eddie, it was difficult for anyone to see things from her perspective. She knew her life would be changed forever, yet she felt that bringing home a baby with special needs wasn't really that different from having a baby perceived as "normal." Every life is worthy of giving and receiving love, she figured, and every life includes challenges. She wrapped her arms around those challenges the moment she decided to adopt Eddie. By bringing home an infant they knew little about, she and Allen committed to this long-term relationship on blind faith, with no strings attached.

This was the deepest commitment the Lees had ever made. It required taking a giant leap into the unknown. Allen cautioned Tilly that Eddie wasn't a car she could return to the dealer. He reminded her that they didn't know anything about the short or long-term challenges, complications, or criticism they might face as a result of adopting Eddie. Allen felt wary, but Tilly felt certain. Indeed, she was fixated on what she saw right in front of her—a new baby whom she would love unconditionally.

In hindsight, I know that Allen loved Eddie, but I also know he felt unqualified to handle the special challenges involved in raising a child with an intellectual disability. Like many people, he had anticipated adopting a healthy baby without complications, especially since they had a choice in the matter.

I was more like Allen than Tilly at the beginning. To be frank, I was somewhat wary of committing to Eddie. Even before I visited him at the foster home in Highland, I questioned how willing I was to get involved. I felt like I was at my limit already, and I wasn't looking to compete with Spider-Man by spinning webs to scale tall buildings in order to help someone else. I had a vague sense that Eddie had been moved from place to place, but I didn't know why and I was reluctant to intervene in decisions that had already been made. My intention was simply to pay him a visit, but that changed as soon as I pulled into the driveway and saw Eddie looking like an unwanted cat that had been thrown out of a car far enough from home that it couldn't find its way back. Despite what I saw, I was also suffused with the reason I wanted to see Eddie in the first place: sheer appreciation for him. Eddie had given me so much to feel good about when I was growing up just by being himself, always eager to share his joy without expecting anything in return.

I got out of the car at the adult foster care home, eager to see if Eddie remembered me. His face was drawn and his shoulders drooped as if he were a potted plant left sitting on the porch just out of reach of rainwater. As we talked, he quickly brightened, infused by our communication with the chlorophyll he needed. Within a few minutes, he looked comfortable and at ease. Before leaving that afternoon, I told him that I would like to visit again and asked if he would like that. "Sounds good to me," he said. "What day?" I threw out the following Wednesday and he followed immediately with, "Okay, what time?" I knew he would be waiting.

From that day on, my commitment to help Eddie became easier, and yet more of a challenge. To cut myself some slack, I decided to do the best I could without promising more than I could deliver. That approach allowed me to respond to Eddie's needs in the moment instead of thinking I needed to solve his entire predicament in one fell swoop.

The following Wednesday, I picked him up as planned. Holding a worn-looking travel mug, eager for a refill, Eddie grinned as I pulled in. When he got into my car, I took one look at the mug and winced, certain it had never been immersed in soapy water, and suggested it was time for a new one. He looked at me like I was taking away his best friend, but after his initial impulse to white-knuckle the mug, he agreed to let me replace it. Before we pulled out of the driveway, I asked if he needed permission to leave, and he told me his caregivers weren't around. Though I'd been told they were looking after him around the clock, I wasn't surprised to find they had other jobs and often left the residents to themselves. The care home was truly passive income.

Our visit started with a quick stop at the small convenience store down the road where Eddie routinely refilled his coffee mug. While he sipped, he told me what he'd like to do on our outing. We started with a few things that I assumed would be quick. After all, I wanted to make sure we had time to buy groceries. As evidenced by his thinness, Eddie had trouble stomaching the food at the care home. Until now, his only opportunity to buy food came when he bought a few items at the corner beer store in exchange for bottle returns.

The first item on Eddie's list was to pick up some bottles and cans a friend was saving for him. Eddie navigated me around the surrounding area, pointing to houses where his friends lived, many from the church he attended. When we pulled into the driveway of a house Eddie directed me to, the garage door opened and his friend emerged as if Eddie held a remote in his hands. Looking as gratified as a raccoon that has just raided a trash can, Eddie darted in and out carrying garbage bags stuffed with returnable bottles and cans. We proceeded to gather more bags from more garages until finally I had to tell him the car was full. I asked Eddie how he carried all these bottles by himself, and he just shook his head and said, "On my bike trailer!" At this, I realized that before his cataracts had become a hindrance, Eddie had covered more territory on his bike in a week than most people did by car in a month.

Time passed, and my trips to see Eddie became more frequent. A week rarely went by without a visit to Highland, but I remained flexible regarding the day in order to work it around meetings and clients. I soon realized that Eddie always carried two lists with him. One was a written grocery list that he pulled out of his pocket and unfolded for me, and the other was a wish list that he recited. This list included trips to the Salvation Army where he scored incredible deals on never-worn clothing, visits to the barber for haircuts, and stops to see friends he wanted me to meet. Visiting his mother was at the top of his wish list. Tilly was now ninety-two and had been living at Argentine Care Facility in Linden for the last six years. She hadn't left the nursing home except for an occasional trip to the hospital since she'd moved in. Linden was forty-five minutes from Highland, and Tilly knew nothing about Eddie's living conditions. I considered telling her how bad it was, but since that wouldn't benefit anyone, I decided to keep it to myself.

Though his visits to see his mom had been rare once he'd moved to Highland, the first time I took Eddie to Argentine Care Facility, I realized it was his second home. From the moment we walked in, every staff member and many of the residents cheerily greeted him, and Eddie dashed in and out of rooms visiting friends and patients as if he were part of the day crew.

We found Tilly sitting comfortably in a recliner next to her bed. We sat and talked for a while, and I wasn't surprised to find she was still sharp as a tack. For the next couple of hours, Tilly and I shared neighborhood stories while Eddie, who never sat still for long, darted out every time he spotted a familiar face in the hallway.

It turned out that Tilly had a list of things she needed help with, too. At the top of her list was cataract surgery for Eddie. It was obvious he couldn't see well, but since he didn't complain, she assumed his other needs were being met. Without his eyesight, she knew he couldn't do the things he wanted or needed to do. His world depended on his ability to ride a bike, and the cataracts were especially limiting due to his legal blindness in one eye. She asked me to help, and though I didn't have a clue how to go about it, I told her I would contact Medicaid on his behalf.

As we spoke further, Tilly began to talk about her frustrations with her immobility, since her physical condition had left her bed-ridden. The air grew heavy when she asked me to locate the money she'd expected to receive from the sale of her house. As much as I wanted to help, I told her I didn't think it was appropriate for me to get involved with locating lost money. It was apparent that her relationship with Rick was strained and that she was looking for a way to get Eddie the surgery he needed. If Rick wouldn't help, she would ask me. It was as if she were saying, "Karen, you showed up just in time. Pull up a chair and let's get to work. I am certain you can help us." During the short time I spent listening to her concerns, I could all but hear the buzzing of an angry hornet coming my way. Without intending to, I had disturbed the nest.

Sure enough, I received a phone call from Rick that evening. His mother had called after I'd left to tell him I'd agreed to help arrange Eddie's cataract surgery. Agitated, Rick didn't hesitate to let me know that I was interfering with the plan he had in place for Eddie and that I needed to butt out. In a lengthy one-way conversation, he explained that he'd tried several times to arrange Eddie's surgery but that, thanks to severe cutbacks to Medicaid, he hadn't been able to.

This was understandable to a degree, but since Eddie was going blind, I told Rick it was unacceptable not to press harder for the surgery. After I offered to help in any way I could, Rick told me that denying Eddie the surgery was the best way to clip his wings and ensure he'd stay out of trouble.

As I listened to Rick's lengthy, well-rehearsed diatribe listing every negative trait he could conjure up about Eddie, I could see he'd become as nimble as a prizefighter. It was clear that he'd been dodging the verbal blows from others who were quick to criticize his care of Eddie and I could tell that he felt frustrated and unappreciated. Burdened as he was with overseeing the welfare of his mother and Eddie, he assured me that he was doing his best. Honestly, I believe he was doing his best, and I didn't have any right to judge whether he was or he wasn't. I simply had a different idea of what might help Eddie, and I was willing to do whatever I could to improve his living situation. At the same time, I could see that while it was easy for others to criticize Rick's actions, they fell short of doing anything that was beneficial for Eddie. Not long after our conversation, Rick came through and made the necessary arrangements so that Eddie could have the surgery he so desperately needed.

Not long after his successful cataract surgery, Eddie was back on his bike. With his vision repaired, he saw every day with the amazement a child displays when looking through a kaleidoscope. Every now and then his eyes would twinkle, he would clench his jaw, and I knew he was feeling happy in the moment—or had just spotted a bottle or can and was marking it with a mental sticky note to retrieve later.

As our weekly outings continued, we visited his mother whenever I had time to take him. Tilly especially liked us to attend the early afternoon activities that got the residents out of their rooms and away from their monotonous daily routines. Most of the residents rarely left the care facility, so these weekly gatherings were well attended. We played Bingo on Tuesdays and sang religious hymns on Thursdays, holidays, and whenever the retired minister and the pianist were available. I wasn't surprised to find that Eddie was good friends with the minister. This was the man who, along with the town barber, had taken him in when his mother's house in Linden was sold in order to buy him time to come up with the money he needed to move into a place of his own.

When Tilly's health began to fail, Eddie and I started making regular trips to the nursing home. Soon she wasn't eating much and was unable to get out of bed, but neither of these issues diminished her lucidity. We sat in her room and reminisced, flipping through her photo album and retrieving things from her storage locker that she wanted to give to Eddie and other visitors. On a cold night in February of 2011, I received a call from the owner of the care center letting me know that Tilly wasn't expected to live through the night. Dennis and I picked Eddie up right away and took him to see his mother one last time. Before she died, as my sister and I had assured her on previous visits, I promised her that we would always take care of Eddie.

My weekly outings with Eddie continued after Tilly's passing. After several months of helping him cash in his bottles, shop at the Salvation Army store, get his hair cut, and make grocery store runs that my sister sent checks to cover, life appeared to be almost normal for him. I was meeting more people he knew, and now that it was spring and he could see better, he was getting around more on his bike. Nonetheless, I was still troubled by his living conditions. When I took him back home after our excursions, I rarely went inside. I preferred to hand him his groceries at the door. I had avoided entering since the day Dennis and I had gone up to his room to see if he needed a new mattress.

We had followed Eddie up the steep dark stairs of the old farmhouse wondering how he hadn't fallen and broken his neck, since this was before his surgery and he was nearly blind. We found that he shared a small, cramped room with no heat source with two other men. Separated by two windows covered with torn plastic, the three small beds placed around the perimeter of the room each held a thin sunken mattress covered with a worn blanket. When I asked Eddie if he was warm enough at night, he said he wore his clothes and coat to bed. He then showed me the rickety metal cabinet he locked his valuables in. He'd scavenged it after catching one of his roommates drinking his cologne.

My reluctance to upset the apple cart came to an end some months after Tilly died. One day, Eddie and I bought so many groceries that I offered to help take them inside. Eddie walked ahead and I followed, placing the bags on the table near the door. The house generally had an offensive odor, but today it was worse. If my childhood memory serves me right, the smell was similar to a homemade stink bomb without the devilishly enjoyable ceremony of lighting one.

It was nearing dinnertime, and I greeted the caregiver's wife as she stirred something in a large pot on the stove. She waved back at me holding a lit cigarette, unwittingly peppering ashes into the pot. In front of me, several small puppies ran around the table, dodging puddles of urine and piles of feces. After I finished bringing in the groceries, I gave Eddie and Noelle a hug and escaped to my car, where it was safe to breathe.

Instead of backing out of the drive, I sat paralyzed, unable to put the car in reverse. Was this the best I could do for Eddie? Was continuing this way giving Eddie's circumstances my stamp of approval? Was I living up to the trust Tilly had placed in me?

I was disgusted with Eddie's living situation and even more disgusted with myself for not having a concrete plan for his future. There was no way Eddie or anyone else deserved to live like this. I lingered in the driveway, unable to move, until I'd decided once and for all to truly help. Before I had time to reconsider, I called Dennis and told him I wanted to help Eddie move out of this house. Always supportive, he immediately assured me he'd help in any way he could.

The next week, I took Eddie to lunch and asked if he would like to move. I had mentioned this topic in the past, but this time I told him we needed to make a decision soon. He answered with an apprehensive yes, and I could see his face flush with fear at the thought of confronting his caregiver with the news. By now, Eddie had been living here for seven long years and was well aware of the house rules. Rule number one was that the caregiver and his wife were the bosses and made the rules and only they could change them.

Eddie's resolve was tested when he told his caregivers he planned to move. In response, they figuratively skewered him on the grill during a backyard barbecue they told him was in his honor. As they feasted on burgers, his male caregiver told him how much they cared about him and how good he had it there. To make matters worse, the caregiver let Eddie know that, if he left, he would be abandoning Noelle. The caregiver then told Eddie that we didn't have good intentions for him and that he'd probably end up living on the street. After that pep talk, Eddie stopped answering my phone calls.

I made a surprise visit and asked him to put aside everything the caregiver had said and focus on this question: did he want to move, or did he want to stay? I told him I understood that this was a hard choice to make given how long he'd lived here.

Not surprisingly, Eddie was torn between his fear that things might get worse and his desire for things to be much better. I reminded him that, as his own legal guardian, the choice was his and that I would understand if he wanted to stay. I also told him that if he wanted to move, Dennis and I would help him find the best possible home. He looked through the windshield at the house for a brief time and then back at me before making his decision: he wanted to move.

Once again, Eddie made the right move. And just like his favorite TV heroes, demonstrate, it wasn't simple. When Dennis borrowed a truck and headed out to load Eddie's belongings for the move to our house, he had a feeling there could be trouble in Dodge. A couple of miles from home, he came across a county sheriff and shared his concern that the caregiver might not be in favor of Eddie leaving. Dennis handed the officers Eddie's identification, and the officer looked at him and asked, "Is this Fast Eddie, by any chance?" Dennis smiled. "Everybody loves Fast Eddie," the officer gleamed, "He's worn out three bikes just collecting bottles."

He went on to explain that the care house was known for questionable activity. There had been some drug overdoses that resulted in deaths but there wasn't sufficient evidence to charge the caregiver, although the caregiver had been in some hot water for selling drugs the house doctor had provided to him under the guise of medical treatment for the residents. The officer gave Dennis his card and told him to call if he ran into trouble. When Dennis pulled into the driveway, the caregiver and his family starting circling the wagon. The caregiver became heated, already feeling the drop in monthly income that Eddie's checks provided, and Dennis pulled out the card and called. Within a few minutes, Eddie and Dennis loaded the truck with garbage bags full of Eddie's life savings and drove away.

In hindsight, leaving the foster home was perhaps the most important decision of Eddie's life. Despite the pressure he felt, he kept his mind on creating a better future and didn't quit. He had become his own advocate, and watching him regain his freedom was worth every hurdle.

5

BE GRATEFUL

"Be thankful for what you have; you'll end up having more. If you concentrate on what you don't have, you will never, ever have enough."

—OPRAH WINFREY

Giving thanks for what we have is easy when we follow our clearly marked calendars that remind us to pass the turkey or when we've got all our ducks in a row. Gratitude requires more intention when it seems our life story is playing like a country western song and we don't think we have diddlysquat. After all, many of us are taught to look at our situations as if we have nothing to do with them—and, worse, as if there isn't much we can do about them. Consequently, we learn to focus on our failures instead of appreciating the valuable lessons we learn from making mistakes.

If only we were assigned to read those books that teach the most important facts of life: that you become what you think, that you create your own reality moment by moment, and that you get better results from thanking than from spanking. You don't have to do much research to find that the greatest teachers and mentors throughout history—think Buddha, Ralph Waldo Emerson, and Wallace Wattles, to name a few—proclaimed long ago that living in a constant state of gratitude creates the perfect platform for success. Indeed, gratitude is the most essential ingredient required to bake your cake and eat it, too.

Many of us just can't fathom giving thanks for our current circumstances when they include credit card debt, student loans, dented fenders, or strained relationships. When life's unpleasant moments have us pinned down like a Japanese beetle in a bug collection, these teachings begin to feel a lot less credible.

However, as soon as we permit ourselves to see past the things that give us ulcers and start appreciating how much we have to be grateful for—even if it's a toaster to put our bread in, a car to drive to work, or a significant other to care about—the wheels of gratitude start turning. Before we know it, our attitude shifts, and suddenly we're creating a whole new perspective. Ask anyone who has pulled success out of a cesspool, and they'll tell you they owe a debt of gratitude to how things lined up once they began showing appreciation for what had happened along the way.

Consider Thomas Edison's gratitude for every one of the thousands of times he failed to create the incandescent light bulb. He knew each failure meant he was that much closer to the golden moment of illumination. If that doesn't convince you, consider what gratitude has done for Eddie Lee.

Eddie ushers in each day like he has just walked out of the auditorium at a Tony Robbins motivational seminar. From the moment he awakens and turns on the television set that sits atop the stand he found at the curb on trash day to the moment he ventures out for a quick walk, regardless of the weather, to see what's new and welcome a day full of possibilities, he's pumped to put the pedal to the pavement. Through it all, he expresses a deep gratitude for everything around him as though it's the first time he's witnessed it. He shuffles up and down the street, waving to cars that pass by and petting neighbors' dogs, as if there's nothing he'd rather do.

Soon after I reconnected with him, I was struck by Eddie's appreciation for things that seemed insignificant to me. As he got into my car and set his travel mug in the cup holder prior to embarking on one of our excursions, his grateful affirmations flowed as effortlessly as water from an open spigot. "Thank God for good coffee," he announced when we stopped at the small convenience store that kept his cup filled for free. "Thank God for good weather," he exclaimed when the rain let up as we drove into the parking lot at Wal-Mart to buy him a new pair of jeans. "Thank God for Reverend Hall. He taught me how to pray," he offered one day completely out of the blue. Honestly, at first I thought he was kidding.

From where I sat, such gratitude seemed a stretch. It was as plain as an old-fashioned donut that Eddie's needs weren't being met. His clothes were filthy, but this hardly mattered since he was lucky to soak in the tub once a week in the bathroom he shared with seven other men. Since he was nearly blind, he couldn't ride his bike and instead spent hours on foot combing the side roads for bottles and cans. On top of that, because his dental hygiene had been overlooked for so long, every single one of his teeth had been extracted. Finally, his mother, his biggest cheerleader and unwavering source of emotional support, was lying in a nursing home unable to do anything for either one of them. But Eddie's positive affirmations were sincere. He could see that life wasn't so bad; in fact, the way he saw it, things were pretty good.

It didn't take long for me to realize that Eddie's habit of expressing gratitude was very effective in shifting his perspective, and I was moved by how it began changing mine, too. We spent precious little time rehashing hurtful things that had been said to him, accusations made against him, or how the caregiver's family scarfed down his groceries before he had a chance to put them in the fridge. There were so many other things on his radar worthy of his attention that he didn't need to relive negative thoughts that took him down a dead end road he had already traveled. Indeed, I was learning that mimicking Eddie's techniques for warding off thoughts of regret, unfairness, and unhappiness were as effective as applying mosquito repellent before going for a walk in the woods.

Above all, Eddie is perpetually grateful for the people who befriend him and treat him with kindness. "Thank God for Uncle John" he proclaimed of a friend who collected bottles and cans for him and, more importantly, was always there for him when he needed someone to talk to. "Thank God for good friends" he said of his acquaintances at church who prayed with him, fed him on weekends, gave him rides to and from services, and never made fun of him or called him names. The gratitude he displayed for his mother topped them all. "Thank God for my mother," he said. "She saved my life."

The more time I spent with Eddie, the more I realized that despite his developmental disabilities and what I'd assumed about his learning potential, he had truly grown. In fact, in many ways, he displayed more mental maturity than many adults sporting Ph.D.s. He demonstrated his remarkable wisdom by using his awareness to focus on things that were pleasing, opening the door to the kind of instant gratification you get from scratching off a winning lottery ticket. Memories of the hurt and anger he'd once felt when being picked on had been replaced with, "Thank God I'm not mad anymore." He had chosen to shed the dead skin of disappointment and grow a new healthy respect for himself without allowing his emotions to be swayed by anyone else's opinions or actions. Eddie had learned to accept the things he couldn't change and supercharge the things he could.

With that shift in thinking, Eddie became a magnet for better things. Bottles and cans seemed to sprout up along the roadside and from the garages of friends like vegetables in a well-tended garden. People offered him everything from rides to church to dinners at restaurants. His positive energy drew my sister back via the article in the newspaper and led her to send him boxes filled with comfort. Their re-opened line of communication eventually summoned me, too.

Although it might be hard to believe, we conjure up the craziest predicaments we get into with the same mind we use to realize our greatest dreams. Every result we experience is an alignment of our thoughts, emotions and actions. This combination creates our vibrational signal and the more we fixate on our current circumstances, good or bad, the stronger the signal we are sending out. The trick is to align ourselves with what we want by thinking it into being, and to continue adding a healthy dose of gratitude as if we already have it; then we can mold the future we want to experience.

Thanks to Eddie, I'm now convinced that as much as complaining might feel like the perfect antidote to everything from hurt feelings to bad refereeing to social injustice, it's about as helpful as eating a tub of ice cream to cure a broken heart—it's nothing but cold comfort. On the other hand, finding the smallest sliver of good in whatever situation you happen to be in is a long-lasting and highly effective pain reliever. Best of all, feeling good leads to better health, better relationships, and a better life.

If the teachings of hundreds of years of wise masters are too old-school, consider the advice of some contemporary counterparts. Jim Carrey and Denzel Washington were busy acting on their dreams before they ever auditioned for the movies that made them block-buster stars. Yes, they worked hard, but their gratitude for every failure was as heartfelt as their gratitude for every accomplishment. Both men realized that gratitude was an essential ingredient in the recipe for happiness and success.

Or take Bob Proctor, co-founder of the Proctor Gallagher Institute. When he was a young man in his twenties, he owed more money than he earned and believed that because he'd been born with a plastic spoon in his mouth, he was doomed to live in debt. Then a mentor restored his faith by placing a different kind of Bible in his hands, the book *Think and Grow Rich* by Napoleon Hill. Following the teachings of this book and using gratitude as a business model, Bob changed his paradigm. Instead of continuing to spew limiting beliefs, he formed a winning attitude. Today, Bob is one of the wealthiest eighty-some-year-olds in the personal development industry and is still traveling the world teaching the secrets of his success at inspiring seminars and coaching events.

Putting her own scientific spin on the power of gratitude, Pam Grout, the author of *Thank and Grow Rich*, invites us to conduct our own experiments with the universe. She discovered the power of gratitude when it seemed her life was on a losing streak. During the seventh inning of her pregnancy, Pam's college boyfriend traded her for a bleached blonde with dark roots. Instead of running to the makeup counter to fix her illusionary beauty flaws and help her compete, Pam applied a different brand of foundation—the teachings of "A Course in Miracles" that taught her to appreciate her inner beauty. Today, her best-selling books offer proof that miracles happen when we expect them to and when we're thankful for what we have.

Eddie came back into my life at a time when I felt lower than an unharvested root vegetable after being practically shut out of the business I had worked so hard to build. At the time, it seemed the best way to get through it was to complain. Even though complaining didn't make me feel better—in fact, it made me feel much worse—people I knew seemed to expect it. Many even offered to rub salt in their wounds by comparing their own hard luck experiences with mine. The only time I didn't feel like I had to explain what had happened and how unfairly I'd been treated was when I visited Eddie. Although he would have listened to every word without judgment, I preferred to hear him rattle off all the good things he encountered and nice people he ran into on a daily basis. We seemed to have an unspoken agreement that every excursion was a scavenger hunt with the goal of spotting as many good things to appreciate or slap our knees and laugh about as possible.

The last thing either one of us needed was negative news. Despite Eddie's circumstances, he continued to display gratitude for the tiniest gestures of kindness bestowed upon him. As I observed this, I began to understand that he had been tapping into his artesian well of inner peace since he was born.

Those of us who think we need to know the secret access code to reach our own artesian wells can stop searching. The code words are "Thank you," and the secret to reaping the greatest benefits is reciting them over and over. As I witnessed Eddie verbalize his expressions of gratitude, it became apparent that he received a surge of energy and gained personal power from the feelings he experienced when he recited these words. Just by coming along for the ride, I benefitted as much as he did. Every trip began and ended with being grateful for his company, and the more time I spent with him, the better I felt—no matter what was going on elsewhere.

Many of us find it difficult to see something to appreciate when it feels like we're lying at the bottom of a mosh pit, but showing gratitude for the worst times as well as the best will keep us from further agony. It may be hard to believe when times are tough, but everything that happens to us good or bad is actually helping us in some way, and if we loosen up enough to notice the message, we can always find something to appreciate. When it seems we never get a lucky break, it might help to stop and consider that each one of us is a living miracle. Scientists have confirmed this by the recent discovery that every single living and breathing human being had a one in 420-trillion chance of being born. We should congratulate ourselves on pulling off such an incredible feat and be grateful for every solitary second we spend here.

Even though Eddie has created a special life, he continues to improve it by finding more ways to appreciate the people who help him and allow him to help them. The more gratitude he expresses, the more good things come his way. The perfect thing about Eddie is that he senses the intrinsic value he offers and isn't ashamed to express himself. Everyone he touches receives the benefit of his positive energy, and everyone he touches remembers him.

On any given day, Eddie spends as much time counting his blessings as he does his returnables. He knows there's a reason things fall into place for him. He also knows that even when things go wrong, something worthy of gratitude isn't far off. Eddie has a talent for zapping negative neurons. The rest of us would be wise to follow his lead, since dwelling on the worst only brings more of the same. We all have the opportunity to live like our glasses are half full rather than half empty, but from Eddie's perspective, there is no halfway when it comes to appreciation because there's something to be gained from both extremes. If you're like Eddie, you drink from the bottle when it's full and cash in on it when you reach the bottom.

6

TREASURE EVERYTHING

> "You aren't wealthy until you have
> something money can't buy."
>
> —GARTH BROOKS

No matter which way you spin the globe, it's clear that since three-quarters of Earth is awash in water, the land we inhabit is actually a flotation device kept in place by a sturdy anchor. This means that no matter what geographic location we call home, we all live on an island. And everyone knows that where there's an island, there's bound to be treasure afoot.

If you aren't easily fooled by the absence of white sand, coconut trees, and thatched roofs, if you aren't expecting a peg-legged prospector with a gold tooth clutching a map and a shovel to point you in the right direction, your chances of finding this treasure are a thousand times greater. As a matter of fact, treasure is always within reach, just waiting to be recognized, created, or thought up.

The problem is, most of us become so landlocked by our beliefs about what treasure is—and even more, by what it isn't—that we walk right past it. As soon as we become friendly with the notion that treasure is everywhere and includes the things we already own, our assets begin accumulating. With an improved mindset, we can align ourselves with even more treasure.

Of course, not everyone has Eddie's special ability to see treasure in things that appear dull, used, and worthless as well as those that shine. He keeps his eyes peeled and his mind open, and with that dynamic duo riding under his bike helmet, he's richly rewarded with treasure that seems to fall into his lap. By following Eddie around the island and observing his techniques, I have discovered a new perspective: that treasure is based wholly upon your judgment. You can choose at any time to see the dandelions sprouting up in your yard as a neighborhood nuisance, or you can see a golden opportunity to make dandelion tea.

Treasure seeking in all its forms has been a favorite pastime of Eddie's since we were young. To him, every day offered the equivalent of an Easter egg hunt because he was always on the lookout for hidden surprises. He stopped by our house on a daily basis sporting something he'd found or been given. "Bet you can't guess what I found," was a familiar greeting. He would then reach into his pocket like he was fishing through the candy-coated popcorn in an open box of Cracker Jacks to get to the prize inside. We were always amazed to see what he'd pull out, everything from a lucky rabbit's foot to a pocketknife he'd found down by the bridge to turkey feathers, arrowheads, transistor radios, pocket watches, matchbooks, or a phone number from someone he'd just met. He was full of surprises, and he loved sharing them.

Since Eddie also loved fishing, he rarely passed up a chance to bring by his catch for us to see. Every catch counted, whether he'd snagged a catfish or been given a goldfish in a bowl. Once in a while, he even caught a whopper. One day, he was particularly excited for us to see the size of the fish he'd just caught. He came barreling from the bridge on his bike preceded by an excited, high-pitched holler. As he flew down our driveway, too excited to pay attention to details, we saw his fishing rod trailing behind his rear wheel, the fish still attached and flopping behind him.

When Eddie grew up, he turned his treasure hunting into a business. During the period that he and his mother lived together in Linden before she entered the nursing home in Argentine, he traversed the streets and side roads on his bike, pulling refundable bottles and cans from the ditches as methodically as a robin plucking a worm from the earth. He cleaned up on his hobby just like his father had profited from finding and selling antiques when Eddie was young.

Eddie's flair for "bottle picking," as he coined it, was both admired and revered. During Linden's Memorial Day festivities in the year 2000, the mayor officially designated May 31 as Fast Eddie Day, celebrating Eddie's contribution to keeping the community clean with a ride in the parade. This pomp and circumstance, of course, culminated in the newspaper article that brought my sister and eventually me back into Eddie's life. And it all started with Eddie's love of finding treasures.

After Tilly was moved into the nursing home in Argentine, about four miles from Linden, Eddie widened his territory, anticipating the new opportunities he had to find treasure on his daily bike rides to see her. When it became difficult to make ends meet, he continued looking for treasure and found it sweeping floors and walking dogs to bring in more money. Even when things bottomed out for him financially, Eddie continued to dig up treasure in the form of love and support throughout the community. He knew that many people cared about him and were doing the best they could to help him.

Although Eddie didn't look forward to moving into the adult foster care home in Highland, it didn't change who he was inside. If anything, Eddie accepted the things he couldn't change and strengthened the faith he had in himself. As a result, he became more aware that his fate was up to him. He truly was the captain of his own ship, especially now that there was no one he could depend on to arrange things on his behalf. Despite being plopped down without a familiar shoulder to lean on in the middle of no man's land where the accommodations were less welcoming than a homeless shelter, he didn't sit and stew, nor did he change his business model.

Eddie went right to work doing what made him feel alive and worthy—finding treasure. He started forming a new network the day he moved in by turning to the first person he met and asking if he needed a friend. Noelle did, and that was that. Next, Eddie got on his bike and resumed prospecting. Like a successful fisherman avoids going home with an empty net, he didn't quit until he found enough keepers.

In Highland, Eddie quickly learned that if he wanted spending money, he had to make it on his own. Bottle picking became more and more important to him, and he became increasingly good at it. Fortunately, the unkempt area surrounding him offered a tremendous opportunity to make ends meet. As a bonus, his hunting skills turned up all kinds of abandoned but worthwhile belongings along the roads and in parking lots. He took these home as well, as if he saw through the dirty exterior of every stuffed animal or misplaced knick-knack or worn piece of furniture to the intrinsic value it held.

In his own way, Eddie's treasure hunting went beyond finding things and into rescuing them; perhaps he felt like he was saving them from being discarded as he felt he had essentially been. He broadened his network of friends in the same way, offering everyone he met a guarantee of his loyalty, respect, and support.

We all know we've come upon something special by the way it makes us feel, yet many of us trip right over treasure and leave it behind without a second glance when it doesn't appear in the shape, size, or color we expect. We've been conditioned to think that everything has to be perfect or that we have to be in some special place or with some specific person before we unearth hidden gems, but all we really need is to be in the right frame of mind. When you're on a mission to find something to treasure, that treasure shows up in the most unexpected places. Like the curious garage sale shopper who leafs through a pile of paint-by-number paintings and drives home with a Picasso, once you add sheer pleasure to your hunting experience, the possibilities of locating something worthwhile are tremendous. The fact is, there is treasure to behold everywhere, and accumulating it isn't limited to reaping piles of money. If it were, bandana-bound pirates the likes of Jack Sparrow would rule the world, and most of us mateys would be tied up in the galley.

Fortunately, regardless of what other treasures we might find, we are all global beneficiaries of the great teachers who have demonstrated that wealth is most valuable when it's shared. Think of philanthropists like Andrew Carnegie, who donated a great deal of his fortune to build libraries in the belief that education was the fertile soil wherein great ideas germinate. By virtue of his own success, Carnegie knew there was a wellspring of potential in everyone. He was so determined to help others tap into their potential that he compelled Napoleon Hill to write *Think and Grow Rich* to lay out the map he and his like-minded contemporaries had used to achieve prosperity.

Philanthropists like Carnegie know something that many others are afraid to accept: that money is a form of energy and that it needs to be circulated in order to create lasting change and greater value. Philanthropists aren't concerned that giving their money away will waste it or leave them broke. They know there's an endless supply of money and that when it's invested in the right causes, it multiplies. Like Francis Bacon said, "Money is like manure, of very little use unless it be spread."

Whether you spend your time on the island finding treasure or digging up excuses to explain why you can't, observing Eddie has taught me that riches are as plentiful as pennies in a parking lot. Everyone can benefit from eyeing treasure from Eddie's perspective, especially on those days when we're hungry for a miracle but feel empty and depleted.

Eddie knows he's come upon a real keeper the second he lays eyes on it, whether it's brand spanking new or has been dropped at the curb on trash day. If it isn't something Eddie can keep, he gifts it to someone else. He sees value and freshness in things others can't, but, most importantly, he maintains this same objective view about the people he meets.

Eddie's curiosity is so authentic that treasure hunting is a daily enterprise. It was undoubtedly his secret to thriving despite being carted off to an adult foster care home that rivaled living on a park bench. He accepted this change as a temporary condition and used the soil surrounding him to resume his prospecting.

Happily, that prospecting has led to treasures that transcend the material. Eddie's world changed the day after his cataract surgery. He looked out the window with amazement and said, "I can see the trees! And the birds!"

After hearing him describe what he saw post-surgery, I felt like I, too, was seeing the world with a level of appreciation I hadn't experienced before. Nature reminds us, and Eddie reminded me, that we are enveloped in treasure that is always before us. Miracles surround us all, but we take many of them for granted. Flowers bloom when the season is right and the sun rises every day without us hoisting it up. It's there for our benefit, even when we fail to see it through the clouds.

After observing Eddie, I've decided that the secret to finding treasure, at least for most of us, is to be more thoughtful about what it looks and feels like. Once we achieve this, we can call off the archeological dig in our back yards because we will know beyond a shadow of a doubt that the greatest source of undiscovered treasure doesn't originate in the material things we seek; it's within every one of us, just waiting to be uncovered and put to good use. No matter what we look like, what language we speak, our level of education, the status of our bank accounts, how many online followers we have, or any of the other limiting judgments we make about ourselves and others, we are all invaluable, individually and collectively.

Eddie is a treasure. Finding him again has taught me to appreciate the true value of this man who was tossed away like a worn rug. He reminds me that every one of us is a gem just the way we are, whether we've been polished in a rock tumbler or washed ashore in the gravel.

He also taught me that when we treasure every relationship, especially the one we have with ourselves, and are willing to acknowledge the value we bring to each other, we are much more likely to encounter treasure wherever we go. At this point, life truly becomes a rich experience because we clearly see that everyone and everything we encounter along our journey has been pointing us in the direction of the spot marked with an X. This is true even when it seems our treasure-finding experiences reflect the kind of letdown endured by Geraldo Rivera upon discovering that Al Capone's overly hyped vault filled with prophesied treasure was nothing more than an echo chamber. Geraldo didn't bury his head in the sand, and neither should we. If we keep looking, we will find the treasure we seek.

Eddie has never used a map or required any sea-faring guide to find treasure. He treasures everything, so, naturally, treasure just follows him home.

BOUNCE BACK

"When life gives you lemons, squirt someone in the eye."

—CATHY GUISEWITE

It seems there is no shortage of sage advice from past and present personal growth gurus who promise that living the life of our dreams is just around the corner as long as we follow our bliss, find our true purpose and go after what we want. Some of us find their guidance so inspiring, we're motivated to abandon our mediocre lives and boldly go where no man, woman or child has gone before. Just when we're pumped enough to jump in with both feet, an undercover bouncer blocks the doorway to our dreams, shooting us that look that says "and where do you think you're going?"

Indeed, the fear of rejection is the very thing that keeps many of us from engaging in the forms of self-expression that could potently make our hearts and pocketbooks sing. For some, it's comfort enough to watch from the sidelines where it's safe and secure, but there are some brave souls among us who are ready and willing to pack their talent and leave their egos at home in order to stand out and pursue their own version of the American dream.

The entertainment industry has wittingly tapped into our burning urge to express our individuality. With a push of the remote, we regularly tune in to a stream of exotic and entertaining programs and promptly become engrossed in watching contestants from every level of aptitude compete, perform, and vie to win the hearts of a panel of discerning judges. Whether they win or are voted off the island, escorted off the stage, or booted out of the boardroom, these courageous contestants have surmounted their fears of rejection. Waiting with bated breath to learn their fate like Dorothy before the great and powerful Oz, they know full well they can't all win, yet they give it their best, knowing in their hearts their efforts will surely lead to something rewarding.

While we sit back in the comfort of our overstuffed chairs watching it all play out in the name of fame, fun, and mostly profit, there is a lesson hiding beneath the cushions. Whether we realize it or not, day in and day out, each one of us stands before our own set of judges looking for acceptance. Every time we apply for a loan, make a friend request on Facebook, try out for a team, interview for a job, apply to college, or any of the other small ways we shoot for the moon, we face being turned down. There is no avoiding rejection unless you're willing to sit on the sidelines watching others go after your dream. The higher we climb in our desire to reach the top of the mountain, the more loose stones we encounter. If we're not careful, these loose stones can send us tumbling into the abyss of low self-esteem. The good news is that we don't have to allow a letdown to determine our self-worth or hinder our ultimate success. As tough as it feels to experience rejection, we can handle it the same way an NBA player handles having his almost perfect jump shot blocked. He doesn't hang his head and head to the locker room in a huff to sell his jersey on Craigslist.

Rejection clears the way for something better. When we keep our eyes open and choose to see this, being rebuffed becomes just another rung on the ladder to success. In other cases, it provides just the impetus we need, even if it causes us to trip on something we weren't formerly aware of. In either event, we don't need the approval of a loan officer, a potential date, or a Hollywood host in order to be happy. In short, we don't need to let the four-letter word that rejection represents—fear—thwart our desire to be our authentic selves. Many individuals feel the sucker punch of rejection first hand, refuse to let it stop them, and find it leads to bigger and better opportunities. When we all do our part by accepting each other just as we are, regardless of talent or title, feelings of rejection don't send us plummeting into hopelessness and depression.

Though Eddie experienced his share of rejection from the get-go, he has never used it as an excuse to give up. In fact, his experiences and especially his response to rejection has led to the extraordinary life he enjoys. He has taught me and everyone he touches that we don't need anyone else's seal of approval to succeed; we can do it our own way and in our own time.

When Eddie and I met as children, it was easy to see that he was too ambitious to be a quitter. Still, it didn't sit well with me that he often endured the sting of rejection because of his intellectual disability. All too often, other people couldn't comprehend his candid and distinctive enthusiasm for life or his need to be accepted and respected for who he was. As the young Eddie poured his heart out to us on our front porch, we were often stunned by the cruel and ignorant ridicule and rejection he endured. It seemed as if many people he met thought individuals with developmental challenges posed some kind of threat and needed to be kept on a tether so they wouldn't place other people in danger or in an awkward position they didn't feel equipped to handle. Often, Eddie made people feel uneasy because he so eagerly extended a heaping plate of acceptance toward them, acceptance he hoped to share a taste of in return.

Similarly, Eddie was often the butt of jokes and name calling with younger people he tried to befriend. He seemed to find this the most hurtful because it was with these younger kids that he felt he shared greater common ground. These experiences hurt, but at the same time, they taught Eddie that he wasn't going to win everyone's approval. He could easily get back on his red hot rod and peel out down the road where friends could always be found. No matter how the rejection originated, Eddie knew that coming to us would help him shake off the experience. Sure enough, as soon as he aired his frustrations and garnered our support, he dusted himself off like a cowboy in a bucking bronco contest, ready to slide his boots back in the stirrups and whirl his hat in the air despite being sent from his saddle into orbit.

What I didn't see way back then was that I was receiving the same solace from Eddie that I was giving him. When I shared my latest letdowns and problems with him with the intention of taking his mind off his troubles, he listened to every word but didn't offer any judgments about how I must have caused my own predicament. This validation was wonderful, since I was contributing plenty of negative self-talk on my own.

Eddie wears the internal scars from his early experiences with rejection well. As much as he knows rejection is part of his personal history, he lives every day without wasting his time looking back. Instead, he continues to write himself a better story. Even though he knows he was all but abandoned as an infant, he doesn't carry the hurt around in his back pocket as a trump card to whip out when things aren't going his way. Eddie's opinion of his biological parents conveys more detachment than anger. Long ago, he accepted that they didn't take care of him. He has invested his energy in feeling grateful that someone else did. Without having to worry about it, he knows that things worked out in his favor. When he was in his late teens, Tilly asked him if he wanted to reconnect with his birth parents, and Eddie quickly declined. What was done was done, and he was happy with the way things were. He knew he had found the perfect parent in Tilly, who supported him no matter what. Tilly didn't hinder Eddie's hankering to go after the things he wanted even though she knew he would experience rejection. She chocked it up to growth and let him learn important lessons the same way the rest of us did, and her approach worked. As Eddie continued to grow comfortable in his own skin, the pestering from the loose-tongued ignoramuses he encountered bothered him less and less.

Nonetheless, Eddie was rocked with a seismic dose of rejection when he first moved into the adult foster care system. Recently widowed and in failing health, Tilly moved in with Eddie's brother, who did not invite Eddie to come along. Unable to understand why there wasn't room for him, the displaced Eddie felt unwanted and abandoned. As if he didn't already feel like the rug had been pulled out from under him, the string of homes he lived in didn't exactly lay down the welcome mat for him. His new caregivers' appreciation for him stopped as soon as they cashed his first check. Eddie found himself living with exactly the kind of people he often rode away from. The caretakers did their share of ridiculing and judging, while Eddie lacked the support and reassurance he had enjoyed in the past. Still, he did his best to fit in and ignore the hurtful treatment he was subjected to. He had nowhere else to go, so he made the best of what he had.

His only consolation was that these foster care homes allowed him to visit his mother whenever he could get a ride. The tradeoff was the accommodations. They were "nasty," to use Eddie's word, and that's probably putting it mildly. Two of the homes were in Flint, a city devastated with economic blight when the auto companies closed the local manufacturing plants and cruised onto the freeway without checking the rear-view mirror. The rejected city was left stunned and in a state of desperation; soon after, crime numbers replaced car production stats as the lead news stories. While he lived in Flint, Eddie's daily walks were short. Many days, he didn't leave the front porch. He spent most of his time doing the same thing his housemates did: waiting for the next meal and looking out the windows. Then one day Eddie took a peek outside and witnessed a murder. As soon as his mother heard that, she insisted on buying a home she and Eddie could share. Her health had improved some and she was able to live independently again. It was smooth sailing in Linden until Tilly's health declined a second time and she had to move permanently into the nursing home. The house was put on the market, and Eddie was sent out into the world on his own. He continued living in the area with the help of his community as long as he could, but when the rent became too high, the only solution was another adult foster care home. At that, Rick drove him to Highland and left.

When I reunited with Eddie, the front seat of my car became the front porch. He didn't share many grievances, but those he did talk about were striking in their similarity to the stories he'd shared when we were young. The only difference was that the people from the past had been substituted with new ones. Sometimes the injustice was something simple, like being left behind while his friend was picked to help cut lawns, but sometimes it was something bigger, like being called "retard" by people he thought he could relate to.

One day as we talked and his mood improved, I realized my recent work-related experiences mimicked unpleasant experiences from my past as well. Though neither Eddie nor I enjoyed rejection while it was happening, it did seem to lead to better things, or at least to different opportunities that were just as satisfying.

I remember confiding my distress to Eddie after I didn't make the cheerleading squad when I was young. As I told him about my seemingly dreadful experience, a revelation hit me like the thud of a medicine ball: I didn't really want to be a cheerleader; I just wanted to make the squad in order to win the acceptance of certain kids at school. This epiphany pushed me to play basketball instead of watching from the sidelines, and I was grateful for the way it all played out. Eddie came to similar conclusions when he met people who didn't accept him or when he tried things that didn't work out. He didn't see these experiences as failures; he just turned towards the next opportunity that popped up.

The reason rejection is harder to swallow than a horse pill is that many of us base our opinions of ourselves by what we think other people think about us. It's natural to want to avoid rejection by our peers—it's why many of us ignore the little voices in our heads that tell us we are worthy and relevant no matter what and that we don't need anyone else's approval to go after what we want. But when we are true to ourselves, rejection becomes a booster shot of adrenaline that bolsters our faith in our own capabilities. Better opportunities and experiences find us when we don't question whether we're worthy of them.

As much as we want to think we live freely, we're taught from a young age to conform, play it safe, and follow the crowd so that we don't get hurt physically or emotionally. Conditioned to accept fear as normal, we follow made-up rules, color inside the lines, and do our best to blend in and camouflage our feelings. We've learned that's the most acceptable, safe, and rejection-proof way to live, yet that's exactly what we *shouldn't* do. We each want to reach our highest potential, and since we all want something different, we have to jump out of line, screw things up, and risk being rejected—a messy process indeed. We are pressured to be politically correct so as not to offend anyone, yet as soon as someone doesn't agree with our views, we reject them personally as if they don't have a right to their own air space. At the exact moment we preach acceptance, we scream rejection.

Meanwhile, we admire individuals who pursue their dreams regardless of how often they are rejected or how many people tell them these dreams are silly or impossible. Take Oprah Winfrey. It's hard to imagine what television, much less the world, would be like without the likes of Oprah. In spite of being told by her first boss that she was too emotional to make it in the business, she wiggled out of the Jell-O mold to become the compassionate talk show matriarch she is. Similarly, Stephen King famously tossed his manuscript for *Carrie* in the trash like a soggy paper towel after it was rejected by thirty different publishers who told him there was no market for his brand of storytelling. Luckily, his wife convinced him to give it one more try.

When I look at how far Eddie has come, it's clear to me that rejection, unpleasant as it is, has played a major role in the success he has manifested. Like a fearless prime time show contestant, he has worked *with* rejection, not against it, except that Eddie doesn't need validation from any well-heeled judge or the "great and powerful" Oz to know he's got talent.

Besides, Eddie and I have both seen *The Wizard of Oz* enough times to know that Dorothy never left Kansas; her solution to rejection was spelled out in living color. All she needed was a refreshing nap and familiar faces to lean on, and then everything looked so much clearer, even in good old black and white.

BE PRESENT

"The main thing is to keep the main thing the main thing."

—Stephen Covey

Now that the once-famous Ringling Bros. & Barnum and Bailey Circus has officially closed the big top and pulled up stakes, the thrilling days of the circus are over. The scores of us who were awe-struck at the dazzling performances by lion tamers, high-flying trapeze artists, and fire breathers will remember the experience forever. As amazing as it was, it's not surprising the circus has run its course, since our taste in entertainment seems to change faster than the screen sizes on our smart phones. Yet for some reason we haven't given up our fascination with the other circus, the one running through our minds.

Despite our good intentions to keep our minds in the same place as our bodies, we race around like chickens with our heads cut off, unsure of whether we're living in the past, the present, or the future. This confusion comes about whenever we catch ourselves in a state of worry or fear. Without realizing it, we relive the past every time we base our decisions or judgments on some long ago or recent event as well as when we begin worrying about the future. We fear that if things aren't going swimmingly today, the pool will surely be drained.

All this thinking leads us to believe we need to assume control of as many facets of our lives as possible, as if this will put us in a better position to catch the sky as it's falling and help us avoid being judged as a total failure. In the process of gaining this control, many of us take on more than is superhumanly possible, hoping to prove our worthiness, our value, and our devotion.

For support, we turn to our most reliable source of protection, that constant stream of feedback that swirls inside our heads, ready to ward off any scary or uncomfortable feelings. This river of thoughts, otherwise known as *mind chatter*, hits us with the force of a crashing wave on open water during a storm. We often get caught up in it, thoughtlessly gushing out opinions of ourselves and others through a constant news feed that provides all kinds of useful information such as *You shouldn't try something new because the last new thing didn't work out so well* or *You shouldn't talk to that person because he looks like trouble*. It's as if we're wearing an in-ear mic that connects us to our own personal negative talk show host.

To make matters worse, and we like to always think the worst, (it is, after all, the responsible thing to do), we mentally dress ourselves as honorary Ghostbusters in an attempt to look more official and qualified for battle and then proceed to prove we're superhuman or at least more eligible, prized, or preferred. All this overthinking and overdoing, glamorously described as multi-tasking, a noble corporate term used to fill in the blank cubicles and create an upside to downsizing, has left many of us feeling overworked, underappreciated, and regretful, not to mention slimed. It's doubly disappointing when we expend our energy in directions that would make Indiana Jones's hat spin only to find that nobody notices, especially when we just cleaned the gutters while bathing the baby while checking our emails while blogging to save the bees while making a slew of sales calls. When all is said and done, most of it could have waited. If it had, the chances are pretty good each task would have been completed more carefully, efficiently, and effectively.

By deliberately slowing down and focusing on the thing we are doing right now, we get more accomplished because we are more able to give each task our full attention without having to play catch up. When we focus, we have a better chance of separating mind chatter from our powerfully productive thoughts. As a bonus, our chances of making mistakes dwindle. Not only do we feel better but also we open the floodgates to accolades for our splendidly complete and accurate work. In other words, we don't throw the baby out with the bath water.

Ever since I started following the basic pointers from Eddie's Eversharp pencil, I've become more conscious of my thoughts and feelings. Being present with myself and more aware of what's happening around me has helped me experience improved results without needing to employ any takedown maneuvers from WrestleMania to trounce my busy mind. Eddie has guided me by his living example, and the lessons, like the benefits, continue to unfold.

Growing up, Eddie's innate gift of savoring every minute flew over my head as surely as he sailed past our house on his bike. He liked to ride by fast, as if he had a propeller strapped to his back, whether he was on his way to town or heading nowhere in particular with the sole goal of goofing around. He was always going somewhere, and sometimes he went with us. But unlike the rest of us, he never asked the question adults liken to fingernails on a chalkboard,

"Are we there yet?" Why would he? He enjoyed the trip every bit as much as the destination.

This isn't to say that Eddie's life was a nonstop carnival ride. He went to school, did chores, served as an altar boy, and offered his services to anyone who would take him up on it. The distinct difference was that Eddie gave everything he did his full attention. In so doing, he found something fun or rewarding in pretty much everything he did.

His keen awareness also helped him notice details that everyone else walked right past. Each spring, he was at our front door with paper bags of morel mushrooms the second they sprouted followed by fistfuls of lilacs the moment they burst into bloom. We quickly determined that it was more fruitful to follow him than to try to beat him to these natural treasures; he was in direct communication with Mother Nature because he was always on the lookout, ready to catch something new or different like an outfielder with an open mitt poised to snag fly balls. While Eddie invested his time rocketing through the streets on his bike, attracting opportunities and letting the fun ones stick like flies to a No-Pest Strip, I was preparing to hop aboard the one-way train of thought that told me my destination as a responsible grown-up required jumping off the swing set, wiping the smile off my face, and getting busy making something of myself.

As a young teenager, I traded a long week from my summer vacation to watch the Watergate trial. I came away wondering why I had to grow up when pillow-fighting politicians elected to run our country were engaging in childish behavior in hotel rooms, pretending to be privileged pin-striped rock stars. As time went on, I joined the millions of others who traipsed off to college only to quickly learn that having fun wasn't included in the curriculum. Like many college kids, I attended without any idea of what I wanted to do, constantly wondering if I was making the right choices and regretting my decisions even before I made them. I was sure that everyone else knew what they wanted to do, but I hadn't a clue as to how this could be possible. I finished school feeling unfulfilled. Even so, I pressed on, thinking that as long as I kept trying to figure everything out, some line of work would eventually suit me. In reality, I didn't think I had time to slow my pace. Life felt like a race, and I didn't want to fall behind and lose. I don't recall engaging in much of anything that was pleasing or memorable.

Long before I saw Eddie again, multitasking had morphed from a mantra to my middle name. I carried around spiral-bound notebooks like a Bible salesman loaded down with lists of things to do, people to call, and problems to fix. When I reconnected with Eddie, I quickly added him to my lineup of responsibilities. As soon as I drove away from the adult foster care home after our first meeting, I went to work figuring out how to fit him into my already overloaded schedule. My first thought was that it wouldn't be possible, since the round trip alone took two hours, but I was promptly overcome by a wave of guilt, the familiar driving force that caused me to make so many commitments.

None of this pressure came from Eddie, of course. He stood in the driveway, happy I had come, without any expectation for anything further except a follow-up visit the next week. Despite everything else I was juggling, the guilt I felt about Eddie's situation began to take a front row seat in my mind. I didn't know exactly how he was being treated, but it was clear things could be better. I just couldn't leave him there without learning more and, if needed, doing something to help.

The following week, I saw Eddie as planned, but I was more present physically than mentally. Although I wanted to see him, there were at three other places I needed to be at the same time. I mentally sprinted through the visit as if limiting my attention and being partially present would make up for what I thought I should be doing. My phone rang the entire time we went from store to store buying Eddie's groceries and some much needed clothing.

Eddie listened patiently to my conversations with clients and subcontractors and good-naturedly put up with the interruptions. Grateful to be along for the ride, he tapped his knee to songs that played softly on the radio while I talked. Each time I finished a call, he would say, "Boy, you sure are busy, Karen. Your phone is ringing off the hook!" I would nod but only to acknowledge he'd said something while I continued taking notes and filling more lines on my to-do list, soberly downloading each phone conversation whenever we hit a stoplight.

As our weekly visits continued, I began to appreciate the change in pace that being with Eddie promised. Each time I saw him, time seemed to slow a little more. I would pull into his driveway, take a deep breath, and shift from drive to patience, determined to put my problems in park if only temporarily. As I chauffeured him around town for haircuts and groceries and to friends' homes to pick up bottles, I slowed down enough to observe him with renewed curiosity. I noticed that Eddie always jumped enthusiastically into the car with his travel coffee mug. Unless I prodded him, he seldom shared any negative details about his living conditions or relationship with his caretakers; he clearly wanted to enjoy himself, and he took keen pleasure in what was happening around him. For example, he liked creating names from the letters he read on the license plates of cars or trucks in front of us, and eventually I joined in with my own. To Eddie, "RPG" stood for "Rick, Paul, George." "STV" was "Steve, Tim, Vector."

"'Vector?' Where did you get that name?" I asked.

"It just came to me!" he replied with a giggle.

We laughed, which prompted Eddie to tell a few of his favorite jokes. Time was different with Eddie. I didn't feel the usual need to race around making sure I got everything done.

Every week the grocery list Eddie pulled out of his pocket read pretty much the same, but as the weeks went by, I became more discerning about what went into the cart. We started to replace his beloved pickled bologna and high-fat potato chips with healthier foods. At the same time, Eddie always took the time to check prices carefully. When he came across a brand of baked beans that cost a few cents more, he'd put it back and choose one that cost less, shouting "That's expensive!"

When I was able to spend the whole day, Eddie and I would visit Tilly at the nursing home in Argentine. As soon as we walked in, my roadrunner speed would slow to the pace of a tortoise. This was not a place where anyone was in a hurry. With the exception of Eddie, who continued to dart in and out of rooms for quick visits with staff and residents, the only traffic came from slow-moving wheelchairs traveling to and from the dining area or to the community room for activities.

On one such occasion, Eddie and I arrived in time for bingo, an activity he and Tilly both enjoyed. We found the community room filled with bingo warriors already set up with as many cards as they could reach, each tenaciously gripping fistful of red and blue chips. Ready to play, I took a few cards, too. Eddie laid out four cards and studied each one closely, memorizing every letter and number. Each time the announcer called the letter and number combination, Eddie scanned his cards, then his mother's, then waited for the residents to check their cards.

To my surprise, every letter and number combination the announcer called was promptly contested or followed by pleas for clarification. If "I2" was called, we soon heard, "Was that N33?"

"Was that I32?" Meanwhile, the residents around us bickered incessantly. "I'm sure he said G13, George." "No, Floyd, listen to what the man said. I heard him. He said G44."

As the afternoon wore on, I looked at Eddie to see how he was taking the growing vitriol, but he just sat patiently shaking his head, waiting for the next number. Soon, I was ready to turn in my chips and head for the hallway before this game of Bingo became a contact sport. This seemingly friendly pastime was becoming a scoreless game of hardball with no runs, no hits, and no end in sight. If it went much longer, we'd be right on time for the Thursday afternoon hymn singing, which at this point was sorely needed. All the while, Eddie remained as calm as a curled-up caterpillar, finishing the game like a champ.

He isn't the only person with intellectual disabilities who exemplifies this sort of patient laser-beam focus on the present. Several memorable individuals with this strength reside alongside Eddie at BrickWays in Traverse City, Michigan. BrickWays is a non-profit organization that provides support to people with disabilities in the form of independent residential housing integrated throughout the community. Hand in hand with their housing comes cooking and housekeeping assistance, employment assistance, and opportunities for personal growth.

Like Eddie, the residents of BrickWays have developmental disabilities, but their antennas are tuned in to appreciating every moment, and they don't seem interested in pushing the pause button on fun so they can complain about how they've been wronged or never get any breaks.

Mary, a long-term resident at BrickWays until her recent death, is a notable example. Despite a rare disability that left her wheelchair-bound, with bones so brittle she broke both legs while attempting to bend over to tie her shoes, she lived happily and fully until she passed at age fifty-five, well beyond her life expectancy. The last year of her life, Mary spent long months rehabilitating in the hospital. Her mother was astonished by her daughter's ability to go with the flow throughout her grueling hospitalization, but Mary's smile never skipped a beat, regardless of the circumstances. She lived every day of her life like it was Christmas and she was St. Nick. Her parents selflessly attended to her needs, and in so doing they improved the lives of many others at BrickWays through the numerous programs they supported.

Eddie, of course, has always reveled in day-to-day pleasures. One of BrickWays' happy and fulfilled residents, he calls me a few times each day just to let me know what he's up to. He tells me exactly what he's doing at that moment, things like, "I'm just sitting here watching *The Rifleman*," or "I'm just sitting here doing some thinking," or "I'm out looking for bottles and goofing off." He doesn't concern himself with what he would rather be doing, with what other people are doing, or with what he needs to do later. He just tunes in to whatever's going on around him. Eddie is a well-seasoned meditator in his own way, and his talent for staying present has a grounding effect on others.

Tim Brick, the son of the founder of BrickWays and the owner of Brick Wheels bicycle shop in Traverse City, tells a wonderful story about the effect Eddie and his friends have on him. "I always think my mother, who was such a jokester, sends her friends around when things are just going crazy—just when you can't think you can't handle any more. I'll have a day when one of my employees calls in sick, my car breaks down, three people are waiting to see me, two more are on hold, and the toilet is flooding. That's when Eddie and his friend Barb walk in and want me to check their tires, or they'll ask if their mirrors are set straight. I just have to laugh because I know

Mom has sent her little helpers to bring me back to Earth. They are my guardian angels."

There is so much to be gained by giving whatever we're doing our full attention, no matter how mundane and unrewarding it might seem. There is always something to be appreciated or noticed in even the tiniest things we do. Those of us who run through our days and nights like our only goal is to check them off our calendars and wish them good riddance lose the entire purpose of being on this giant playground called Earth. Sad to say, no matter how attractive, cute, or inspiring the calendars or planners, most of us equate Monday through Friday with work and consider them giant blockades to freedom until the weekend. It takes vacation time for us to forget our schedules and enjoy ourselves. Even then, many of us become vacation warriors. Fearful of missing something or of being considered expendable, we check emails and make phone calls until we end up without much down time at all.

The truth is, there is nothing more important than what we are doing right now, at this exact moment. This isn't to say we can't dream about the future or recall the past—there is time for everything, as long as it doesn't clog our ability to focus on what we have in front of us. Being present makes even the least pleasant tasks we engage in more rewarding.

If you're like me, you will be pleasantly surprised at how much better you'll feel if you can begin to appreciate this truth. You will become more in touch with yourself and will gain a whole new appreciation for the things you do. You'll also find that approaching every day with this powerful attitude improves your life significantly because being present helps you appreciate the nuances all around you.

A license plate you spot on the street could spark a nice memory. A brief encounter could clarify a question you've been pondering. A cloudbank shaped like Yoda could provide a reminder that the force is with you.

Eddie might have had a hard landing upon arrival, but he got up and rode off in one piece. In large part, I believe this is because he tunes into how he is feeling moment by moment and lets life unfold in front of him. His mental chatter is minimal; there are no wild circus animals running loose in his mind. He tamed them long ago.

INCLUDE YOURSELF

"Unless someone like you cares a whole awful lot, nothing is going to get better. It's not."

—Dr. Seuss, *The Lorax*

Every time the driver of a Jeep Wrangler crosses roads, mountain paths, or parking lots with a fellow Wrangler driver, something happens that reminds them both they're part of an exclusive tribe. No matter the color, age, or condition of the drivers or the vehicles, the drivers exchange what's known as "the Wrangler wave."

This simple hand gesture might look as silly as a knock-knock joke to others, but it sends a signal that the two drivers have something in common worth noting. Paint colors aside, there is no "black Jeep" of the Wrangler family.

The question is, why do they do it? I have perused the operator's manual, and unless I'm missing an asterisk followed by tiny type, nothing says that friendly hand gestures made while passing a vehicle of the same make and model will result in better gas mileage or prevent road rage (though it no doubt will help with the latter).

I believe the answer lies in inclusion. We all want to belong to something bigger than ourselves, and we feel a tremendous sense of pride and acceptance when we're included. When we come together to find and appreciate our similarities, our differences offer the contrast that teaches us the most about ourselves.

We don't have to dust off the old Funk & Wagnalls encyclopedia to recall instances when we fist-bumped a foe or two and put our differences aside for the good of all. Opportunities to care, offer support, and reach out to others we think are different from us often appear in the face of tragedy. On September 11, 2001, our spinning planet came to a screeching halt long enough for surveyors to remove the boundary irons that border Manhattan and pound them in on the other side of the globe. Visibility might have been low at Ground Zero, but from the first responders to the outpouring of support from neighbors around the world, it was clear that we are one community and, further, that we are responsible for each others' welfare. Even television news stations showed their solidarity and displayed a moving banner across every screen with an up-to-the-minute report showing the number of lives lost and bodies newly recovered.

We felt compelled to remember these people who died in the buildings and fell from the sky because they were our family members, friends, and co-workers. They were us—regular people going to work, attending appointments, or traveling by plane. It's easy to come unraveled when tragedies of this magnitude occur, but we don't. The worst times bring out the best in each of us and ultimately, we are reminded that we are on the same team when unthinkable events occur. We learn the most about the importance of building strong communities when tragedy strikes. Always, we limit our potential when we shine a spotlight on differences and make decisions based on fear.

Most of us tend to think of community as the network of people we encounter in the places we live, work, worship, and spend most of our time. This is true to some extent, but community actually starts closer to home, since each of us is a community unto ourselves. It's good to be reminded that we are made up of roughly fifty trillion cells and that every one of them is working on our behalf around the clock. With that kind of support group, you would think nothing could stop us, but the minute we see ourselves as incomplete or inferior, we invite a whole community of fear to assemble and take control. I learned from Eddie that it serves us all better—it serves us all best—to include ourselves and reject the notion that inclusion hinges on meeting the approval of others to decide whether or not we fit in.

In reality, we are all a perfect fit and deserve to be accepted and included just as we are. Of all the lessons my father taught me growing up, inclusion was paramount. Dad owned one of three bars in our small town, and provided a service to the community that some didn't understand. He listened to his patrons more than he filled their glasses, and became friends with many that weren't accepted by others. The first time Dad announced that he was bringing Frank, the town drunk, to our house for Thanksgiving dinner, we thought he was off his rocker. We soon discovered that Frank was just as nice as anyone else we knew, and looked forward to sharing more holidays with him. If only more people knew that Frank was a war veteran who suffered from emotional wounds that only alcohol could soothe, he may have been treated with more understanding; but back then, post-traumatic stress disorder was undiagnosed.

Eddie and I grew up about a mile and a half outside the small town of Carson City, Michigan. My family only had one car, so I felt a bit isolated from my friends who lived inside the city limits and routinely walked back and forth to each other's houses. My siblings and I found a way around this calamity by developing our own neighborhood friendship circle. Since I am blessed with six siblings, my brothers and sisters made up a significant portion of the circle, but everyone who showed up was welcome. This club became our before-school, after-school, and weekend community, and it was flexible and talented enough to transform into a baseball league, hockey league, swimming club, or abandoned house and barn spy club at any moment.

Tellingly, Eddie's sense of community stretched much further than ours. He didn't feel confined by distances, so he rode his bike wherever he pleased, enjoying the journey so much that he rarely reached his destination. Once in town, he used his time to stretch his community even more, often bringing back trinkets and tokens from newly formed friendships. He volunteered at church, helped bag groceries at the store where his mother worked, and generally pitched in whenever anyone needed a helping hand. He joined our group whenever he felt like it, but—again, tellingly—we felt protective of him whenever anyone outside our neighborhood nucleus stopped in. We didn't know just how much territory Eddie covered, and we were unsure that others knew about and accepted his disability. Once again, Eddie taught us that he carried his own weight through his positive and caring attitude, his sense of adventure, and by always being his authentic self. Consequently, he helped us all grow into the accepting individuals we are today.

Ever since we were reunited, Eddie has expanded my sense of community well beyond the boundaries I've set for myself. Working with him has triggered my biggest growth spurt since my wonder years while expanding my family's understanding of what community really means Our reunion pushed me to venture into uncharted territory that felt uncomfortable at first, but the more I let go of worrying about having a solution to every problem, solutions appeared in amazing ways.

Once I became part of Eddie's continually expanding family along the bike trail from Argentine to Linden to Highland and ultimately to Traverse City, I saw that in each place he lived, Eddie was welcomed and supported by the town barbers, pastors, storeowners and employees, fast food employees, nursing home staff, church members, Salvation Army staff, police officers, and others. One family paid special attention to Eddie, letting him call their two children his grandson and granddaughter. I met many of these people during our road trips. I think in part Eddie wanted me to know that he was supported, but I also think he simply wanted to include me. Eddie's beloved community gave him faith, and everywhere we traveled, it became clear that faith has guided him safely through every predicament and helped him accept and adapt to every situation he's found himself in.

As a child, I used to wonder what would happen to Eddie when his mother died. For a long time, I assumed it was up to someone else to figure out. Then Eddie and I became reacquainted. When I saw that Tilly was nearing the end of her long life, I realized that Eddie might well live the rest of his in a distinctively unpleasant and unhealthy adult foster care home if someone didn't step in. Consequently, I borrowed a page from Eddie's hymnal and sang along, knowing that he always seemed to come out on top.

It turned out that Eddie and his mother had a plan, one they had been working on for a long time. They simply let the dots connect themselves by being a part of the community everywhere they went. When they needed it most, they simply opened their hearts and invited the community they'd established to help, and their prayers were answered. The universe is wildly accommodating when we participate and proceed with faith and perseverance. The minute we set Eddie's move from the adult foster care home into motion after Tilly's passing, the stars began to align to guide us all through the transition.

After leaving the home in Highland, Eddie moved in with Dennis and me while we searched for a new home that would fulfill his needs. As we began reaching out and exploring possibilities, we learned about BrickWays in Traverse City. Even though our family had vacationed in northern Michigan for several years, we were initially unaware of the extent to which this remarkable community provides support for people with developmental disabilities.

Traverse City once housed the Traverse City State Hospital, which opened in 1885 and was dedicated to the care of individuals with a myriad of special needs, some physical, some developmental, and sometimes both. The state hospital housed and treated patients from all over the state and took in patients from other state hospitals as well. Funding cutbacks began in the 1970s, with services continuing to dwindle until the facility officially closed in 1989, leaving many in need without a care facility.

The residents of Traverse City had long accepted the state hospital as a vital part of their community. It touched the lives of people close to them and employed many local residents. As it began to flounder, one local citizen took it upon herself to fill a need for those with developmental disabilities that the hospital and other programs couldn't provide.

Mary Jean Brick was a lifelong resident of Traverse City. She had grown up with a sister with special needs and had developed a unique ability to care for and understand individuals with disabilities early on. Then Mary Jean's oldest son, John, was deprived of oxygen at birth. Although John developed typically early in his life, the trauma he experienced eventually triggered a nervous breakdown that evolved into a mental disability by the time he reached puberty. It was then that the Brick family began its sobering connection with the state hospital. Through John's experience with treatment there, Mary Jean realized that many people were not receiving the help they needed through the limited services the hospital setting provided. Unable to rest until she'd found a way to offer a life of fulfillment and purpose to people with disabilities, she founded BrickWays, where Eddie now lives.

Mary Jean's goal was not merely for the community to accept individuals with special needs; that would have been too simple. She worked passionately to build her community around individuals with developmental disabilities so that each of them would have the opportunity to actively pursue their passions and enjoy their special roles as thriving members of the community. She didn't want these individuals to fit in; she expected them to stand out and be recognized and appreciated as the unique individuals they are. When it came to finding a place in the community for them, she didn't mind playing matchmaker. It was perfectly normal for her to walk into the hardware store with one of her BrickWays residents, pick up a broom, and hand it to him while she addressed the store owner with something like, "Frank, this is Tony. He will be working with you today, sweeping your floors. I will be back to pick him up at five o'clock." Mary Jean's vision has become a model for organizations around the country that provide services and support for individuals with developmental disabilities.

Beyond her activism and advocacy, Mary Jean Brick is remembered for her sparkling sense of humor. In her own lighthearted way, she taught many people that when we loosen up and let go of our judgment and illusionary beliefs, life improves for everyone. She invested herself in causes that reminded her community that everyone deserves the same opportunities for self-fulfillment, but she gauged her assessment of fulfillment on whether or not the people around her felt connected and happy and were having fun. Mary Jean knew we weren't born to suffer, as that would be a waste of time and effort. She lived her life with fun as her purpose, so it was easy for her to see that anyone who wasn't having fun wasn't living his or her purpose. Encouraging everyone she touched to get back on the playground and climb the monkey bars alongside her, she used fun as her platform to gain the support of the community she lived in.

Mary Jean Brick was also admired for her fearless actions on behalf of those who were typically perceived as less fortunate and for showing others how deceptive this perspective was. Once, to drive this point home, she attended a party masked as a disfigured woman. When acquaintances awkwardly shied away, unsure of how to behave, Mary Jean removed her mask and schooled them on their prejudice. She didn't do this to embarrass anyone; her goal was to challenge their limiting beliefs so that they could begin to question their own judgments and behavior.

I never met Mary Jean, but I've been a privileged student of Eddie's twice now. The second time, I was moved to the front row of the classroom so that I could pay better attention. I thought I'd learned all I needed to about individuals with developmental disabilities growing up. I thought that acceptance and understanding were all they needed to feel like they fit into the community, but I was wrong. Channeling Mary Jean Brick, Eddie and his friends at BrickWays have shown me that every one of us has something unique to contribute, that our talents as well as our needs are different, and that we all need and deserve to be appreciated and respected. In addition, I've learned that those with intellectual disabilities are thoroughly capable of speaking for themselves. We often think that these individuals can't make good decisions without the assistance of a "normal" adult, but this thinking is entirely flawed. If we pay attention, our differently-abled citizens become our best teachers and mentors because they ask us to look at ourselves and to challenge our standard way of thinking.

Truth be told, many of us would benefit from challenging the way we think. In addition to underestimating the abilities of those with special needs in our communities, we take much for granted when we assume that helping care for them is someone else's responsibility. Taking that responsibility on ourselves isn't necessarily simple—there's no phone app to tell us when it's time to assist someone who needs understanding, a ride to the store, or a monetary donation. We frequently feel unqualified to engage with others, especially those with special needs. More often than not, we're afraid to get in the middle of something that could bring judgment upon us. The question is, how temporarily uncomfortable are we willing to be in order to help?

We can take a lesson from Eddie and his friends at BrickWays, who would be glad to show us the ropes. They can be counted on to step in whenever they see a need, anything from cheering someone up to showing up to volunteer to mediating a conflict or misunderstanding. Eddie and his posse of friends Rob, Mary Jane, Bob, Barb, James, Kenny, and Dylan can often be seen consoling other residents who are having a bad day or finding it difficult to recover from the loss of a parent, a sibling, or a pet. First in line to volunteer at events throughout the summer season in Traverse City, they are welcomed at the Cherry Festival, the Traverse City Film Festival, and every other event that needs help.

The Traverse City area is a widely renowned northern Michigan vacation favorite, but it offers services that stretch far beyond the beauty of the natural landscape. It's a community rich with entrepreneurs who find a way to build businesses and organizations that support and include those with special needs and abilities. Three exceptional examples are Grand Traverse Industries, PEACE Ranch, and Arts for All of Northern Michigan.

Several of the BrickWays residents work at Grand Traverse Industries, a private nonprofit corporation that has been providing job placement and employment since 1974 through a variety of production, custodial and assembly positions. The president, Steve Purdue, and his staff know every employee and tailor their work assignments based on their individual needs, making inclusion and advocacy their top priority.

Providing emotional support for those in need, PEACE Ranch is a 501c3 charity that offers a special healing therapy that treats individuals who suffer from trauma, abuse, neglect and loneliness through Equine Assisted Psychotherapy. It began when founders Jackie and Paul Kaschel welcomed three children into their family who had been "rescued" by local authorities after suffering severe neglect and abuse. The emotional wounds were so deep that every traditional treatment option they tried wasn't giving their children the relief they needed. That's when Jackie discovered the unique healing power of horses. PEACE Ranch offers services at low or no cost for disadvantaged populations. Their programs are designed to help individuals reach a new level of healing by bonding with specially rehabilitated horses.

For the past fifteen years, Arts for All of Northern Michigan has been empowering people with disabilities through a wide range of art programs. Grace Hudson and her team of accomplished artists have designed special programs for them using music, dance, drama, creative writing and visual arts. These programs are bolstering self-esteem and encouraging creative self-expression to thousands of children and adults with special abilities.

Eddie and his friends find support wherever they go in the community. From the police officers, churches, and friends who shower Eddie with large bags of returnable bottles and cans, the Traverse City area is filled with people who appreciate the tremendous value these individuals offer.

Not long ago, my husband Dennis and I attended a memorial service for the father of Barb, Eddie's special friend and fellow resident at BrickWays. With her sister by her side and the encouragement of her deceased brother Mark within, Barb delivered a eulogy that began, "It wasn't easy raising a child with developmental disabilities." She continued to address us mourners in her open and honest style, celebrating the life of a man who clearly appreciated his daughter's wisdom and honesty.

Barb is an exceptionally thoughtful woman. She explains that she sometimes forgets to makes sure she has money in her account before she writes checks. She'll be out shopping, and low and behold, finds something one of her friends needs, and pops for it. Indeed, sometimes her pocketbook isn't as bountiful as her heart, but she has plenty of support to help her get back into the black.

Faith helps, too. Eddie's faith has played a big role in his life since he was young and has always helped him create community. He was raised in the Catholic Church, but today he doesn't pay any attention to the denomination, nor does he concern himself with memorizing prayers or hymns, although he would gladly sing along to any Elvis Presley tunes the pastor might want to include. He attends the church that looks nice and always seems to find those that offer the perfect balance of fellowship and food. When Eddie lived in Highland, the church he attended provided him with much needed emotional support, while the weekly after-service meals offered his best chance at a healthy plate of food. He has always felt that church is a safe haven, a place where he is accepted for who he is. Having carefully observed his favorite pastors over the years, he now enjoys sharing his faith by conducting his own prayer sessions with friends.

Eddie knows intuitively that each one of us is a community unto ourselves. The further we stretch our own limits and the more we connect with others, the more we form the kind of fellowship we're all seeking: a community as tightly knit as Spandex, where we're so focused on all that we have in common that our differences become admirable rather than negligible.

That's the kind of thinking that encourages and supports positive growth because it allows every individual to thrive. Each of us has something in common with one another, yet we all arrive with our own one of a kind thumbprints. Eddie knows this. He is the ultimate community organizer, and he does it without an official job title, his business cards notwithstanding. He has spent his life perfecting his purpose. In so doing, he has taught me that life really is like a ball of Play-Doh; it's up to each of us to make something fun out of it.

Every Friday, I get a call from Eddie telling me he's on his way to unload the food truck at the church. "I haven't volunteered for a while, and I want to help out," he'll say. Then he'll add, "And they have good coffee." If he's not volunteering, he's checking in on his friends at Brick Wheels. He loves to stop in and look for more ways to add bling to his red hot rod and say hello to the staff and his special friend Tim Brick, whom he says, "is like an uncle to me."

From there, he goes to work at Right Brain Brewery, where Russ and his crew provide the perfect space for Eddie to shine. He washes glasses, clears tables and contributes to the uber positive atmosphere that's always on tap there along with some stellar craft brews.

Eddie wakes up every morning feeling as lucky as a leprechaun. He credits his success to the countless people in the every community he's been part of over the years who have offered their support and treated him like family. The list is vast, and though at times he occasionally forgets a name or two, he remembers every kindness he's ever received.

He returns that kindness tenfold. Even though he doesn't drive a Wrangler, Eddie has his own hand-waving habit that comes into play whenever he gets behind the handlebars. He waves at those who ride bikes and at those who don't, at those who wear helmets and those who do not, at people who drink from cans or bottles, and at pretty much everyone else.

Imagine what our world would be like if we all waved back.

10

Be HAPPY

"I'm just happy being happy."

—Fast Eddie

In a perfect world, the chances are good that we would be living in a constant state of bliss. Imagine what that would be like: We wouldn't feel the need to improve anything about ourselves, nor would we need to expect others to improve themselves in order to please us. Our burgers would always be served just like we ordered, our kids would all be away at college on four-year scholarships, the fish would always bite, and our dogs never would. Life would be grand.

The thing is, we can experience happiness anytime despite any imperfect outer conditions. The contrasts we encounter daily offer us more reasons to be happy than we realize. But since many of us believe that happiness is an all or nothing game, we devote a great deal of time and effort seeking it out—we jump on the interstate and Internet highways on a full out search. We collect as much as our trunks and charge cards allow and we cruise cheerfully along until something that resembles a pothole, like a bad report card, a broken bone, or a sandwich sans the cheese we clearly ordered causes a rattling noise we can't ignore, no matter how high we adjust the volume on the radio. This chain reaction serves as a painful reminder that there is only one place we can buy happiness; so we get off at the first available exit, pass the bump shop and belly up to the bar in time to settle for a shot of it at a reduced price for an hour.

Even though we know we can get through even the most devastating circumstances and prove it every day, many of us feel obligated to loop together a daisy chain of disasters by which to define our days. Perhaps we want to justify our feelings of disappointment by connecting them to various unfortunate events that derailed us in the past. As much as we don't like to feel unhappy, we weave together a sad saga whose theme is that we somehow deserve to suffer. Then we get as much mileage out of this narrative as we can, inviting others to join in as if making them feel worse will make us feel better. This is the biggest reason we're ready to cry uncle at the slightest hiccup instead of seeing things that happen as mere events we can recover from quickly, chalking them up to lessons learned on the road to success.

Maybe we allow our happiness to be fleeting because ever since our mouths were plugged with pacifiers, we swallowed the belief that in order to experience true happiness, we had to earn it, buy it, fight for it, win it, or inherit it. As awful as it feels to feel bad, we accept it as normal and appoint it as our navigator, handing over the keys as we ride along in the passenger seat, our happiness stored in the trunk next to the spare tire, waiting for conditions to become more favorable before we conclude it's safe to feel good again.

Many of us don't realize that happiness is easier to come by than popcorn on the floor of a movie theater once we understand that it's not only safe but highly advisable to feel good. We also tend to forget that feeling good doesn't require any special equipment, a given amount of money, or improved conditions. Since we actually generate happiness, it would be a good idea to stop expecting it to come from someone or something outside of ourselves. We are all absolutely perfect just as we are, blemishes, addictions, mistakes and all. What's more, if there were such a thing as a personal owners' manual, we'd see that we're never instructed to feel happy later because we don't quite deserve it yet.

As always, I learned this from Eddie, who is keenly aware of the most important aspect of his sole guardianship. Whenever he feels the hair rise at the back of his neck because someone is barking orders at him or criticizing his ideas or actions, he dials me up and proclaims in a huff, "I am the boss of me!"

Eddie is right. He knows that his feelings are his greatest source of power, and when he feels challenged, he becomes infused with the same strength as Superman emerging from a phone booth in full costume.

This goes for the rest of us, too. Despite the fact that many of us run around thinking we're no better off than corralled cattle under the control of our managers, teachers, parents, mortgage lenders, the government, and the list could go on, each one of us is our own boss. Period. That is simply because nobody else has control over our feelings. No matter who tells us to stop giggling, smirking, or crying, changing our outward expression doesn't change how we feel inside. No matter what happens to us or around us, we choose whether to feel happy or sad, critical or compassionate. Our emotions determine the way we experience the world, and, without question, they are the most reliable prognosticators of our future reality.

There is never a bad or inappropriate time to feel happy. When we write our fairy tales with a version of happily ever after that ends in conditions like *When I get an apology*, *If I get a ring*, *When I get the raise*, or *If we win the championship*, we choke off the flow to our true potential and everlasting happiness just as surely as a kinked hose cuts off the water supply.

It feels so much better to be surrounded by uplifting, positive news that many of us now go out of our way to put controls in place that limit the amount of banter, negative or otherwise, we allow between our ears. At the push of a button, we can change the television or radio station or filter the news we see on social media. But it turns out that the bulk of our input arrives in a continuous feed that begins running the day we are born. Our subconscious minds act like the black box in the cockpit of a plane, recording every bit of data we receive from those around us. This is a problem because we end up picking up information from a smattering of opinion polls that includes our families, friends, business associates, and the media. We gather this information without judging whether it's good or bad, and since we turn to it when forming our opinions, we end up putting a lot of stock in what others think. The answers to our most probing questions come faster than pop-up ads on the Internet. Unless we block them long enough to question their validity, we end up allowing the opinions of others to influence whether we think we're good enough, smart enough, or deserving enough to do what makes us feel good.

When we don't get a handle on these thoughts, we end up making choices based on a set of analogies stored in the vault of someone else's limiting beliefs. When we allow others to control our feelings by telling us if and when we should or shouldn't feel good, we put our future in someone else's hands. Then when our simplest wishes fail to materialize or don't look exactly the way we expected them to, we feel let down and undeserving of better.

Meanwhile, we toil long hours at work so that we can afford to buy what we think will make us happy. Once we have our eye on just the thing that will shift us from boredom to bliss and are willing to pay just about any price to get it, we expect happiness to arrive in a box on the front porch using standard delivery—even faster if we pop for express shipping. Product developers and advertisers keep up with our insatiable hunger for products that will fill the voids in our hearts by coaxing them into our shopping carts, driveways, and medicine cabinets. They've done the research, so we trust them to tell us what to buy. We're desperate to feel happiness, or at least temporary relief from unhappiness, yet we often demand concrete evidence that something will make us happy before we buy into it. That way, we won't waste our efforts or our time. We do this because we've been taught that to experience happiness without a purpose would be a killjoy, but nothing could be further from the truth.

It turns out that happiness without purpose is the meaning of the whole game. In fact, we are incapable of experiencing real and lasting happiness as long as we hold onto the belief that we will be rewarded with happiness only after we get what we want.

A weekly dose of Eddie's elixir of glee was all it took to bring me back to the understanding that happiness is homemade and doesn't require refrigeration to keep it fresh or preservatives to extend its shelf life. Each week, even before I drove up Eddie's driveway at the adult foster care home, a familiar good feeling bubbled up inside me.

I would recall how, as kids, Eddie's happiness had flowed in an endless stream down the road to our house, his cowboy-quality hoots of "Yee-haw!" ricocheting throughout the neighborhood like high noon at the O.K. Corral. The smallest bluegill on his fishing line garnered the same seismic outburst as a trip to Disney World. Eddie never categorized the degree of joy he expressed according to size or shape. He was so consistent in his belief that happiness was his right-hand man that he never let himself feel disappointed for long.

Despite the image of Eddie I retained from childhood, once I saw him again as an adult, I struggled to believe he was authentically happy. I didn't see how he could be, given his degrading circumstances in the adult foster care home and his inability to see or ride his bike. I didn't realize it at the time, but I doubted happiness was possible in such a setting. In retrospect, I was sizing up his unhappiness based on mine. I wasn't feeling so great about my own letdowns, so I figured he couldn't possibly feel good about his.

I adamantly believed that Eddie didn't want to face how bad things were for him in Highland—either that or he had downgraded his notion of what happiness was. During our initial road trips, I carefully quizzed him, certain he must be covering up his true feelings, but Eddie didn't want to engage in my "Inspector Clouseau" line of questioning. Typically, he promptly switched the subject matter to something more pleasing to him, rendering my hat and magnifying glass useless. Eddie didn't go through a lot of Band-Aids anymore, I finally concluded. He wasn't one to reopen old wounds by being spiteful or wallowing in hurt; his way of healing was to peel out on his hot rod, leaving nothing but tire marks and dusty, useless remarks behind. Any comments he made about the way he was being treated at home were minimized and dissolved as quickly as an Alka-Seltzer tablet dropped in a glass of water.

Eddie's positive attitude caught me off guard, and I wasn't the only one. Many people he approached during our weekly outings, from store clerks to shoppers to barbers, found themselves using facial muscles they hadn't exercised in a while. By the time Eddie finished greeting them, their teeth sparkled behind their upturned lips like they'd just left the dentist's office after a perfect check-up. I became accustomed to walking slightly behind Eddie to capture the full effect of his hypnotic charm, but I admit that the first time he approached a sad-looking woman pushing a grocery cart at a

Wal-Mart, I had to stop myself from stepping in and explaining Eddie to her.

Wait a minute, I thought, coming to my senses. *Eddie doesn't need explaining, and what would I say anyway?*

The woman's response to Eddie's greeting was priceless. His genuine concern as he tapped her on the shoulder, looked into her eyes, and asked, "Hi, I hope you're having a beautiful day!" changed her expression completely, like she had just won a prize teddy bear at the county fair. She was a blessing to Eddie, too, because when he helps someone feel better, he illuminates like a lighthouse beacon.

Studies show that happy people are generally healthier, enjoy better relationships, and are more likely to be successful. Knowing this, you would think that making the conscious choice to be happy would be at the top of our to-do lists, but many of us defer to our internal mental programming. More often than not, that voice is like a drill sergeant with a megaphone, shouting at us to fall back in line whenever we feel the urge to have a little fun. In addition, we are conditioned to believe we shouldn't be happy because it would be unfair to the people who aren't.

This assertion isn't unfounded—many individuals have a negative reaction to happiness. If you've experienced what's it's like to feel passionate about an idea and fully invest yourself in bringing it to fruition only to have a well-meaning friend drown your enthusiasm with their own fears or negativity, you know what I'm talking about.

We need to shrug off such experiences secure in the knowledge that humanity's best innovations come from decidedly happy people who are willing to face their fears and follow their hearts. When happiness and optimism end up at the bottom of the pile of priorities, weighted down by obligations, why not pause, start over, and approach those mundane tasks with the same positive attitude we invest in the things we love to do? All our tasks will become more rewarding, and our chances of finishing each one will become greater, too.

As much as we wholeheartedly mean to focus our energy on being happy, we deny ourselves joy on a regular basis. Recent studies attest to the fact that most Americans aren't getting any happier in spite of an improved economy, rising incomes, and abundant Seinfeld reruns. Look no further than our current health crisis to see the truth of this. Never mind the daily medical breakthroughs that promise cures to illnesses that just yesterday were hopeless killers. As a nation, many of us aren't feeling so good. The more science steps up to fix our aches and pains, the more new diseases we invent. Literally aching to be happy, many of us complain that the medical profession is corrupt even before we reach the doctor's office. Then we call out the pharmaceutical industry for the outrageous price of drugs. We finish it off by labeling all health insurance carriers evil.

But here's the kicker: we can be so out of touch with our emotions that we don't stop to question what's really bothering us, and more importantly, why we think we need to validate our bad feelings by holding on to them. We wear the negative emotions of yesterday's hurts like bad tattoos, demanding answers from doctors and pharmacists to help us to feel better as though our well-being is entirely dependent on them. If a doctor tells us we're making ourselves sick with worry, anger, or other unhealthy habits, we search for a second or third opinion to tell us what we want to hear.

What most of us really want is to leave the clinic with a miracle pill even before the tests have come back from the lab. For some reason, it makes us feel better to trade megabucks for milligrams in order to confirm that our sickness is real and isn't just in our heads. This is a big mistake because sickness starts where we stand. Just like the arm bone connects to the wrist bone, our thoughts connect to our feelings, and too many of the negative ones can make us sick. We contribute to the problem by highlighting our negativity and communicating it to others. At every given moment, we send out vibes that convey either our desire to trade, copy, and compare complaints or to swap peace signs, hugs, and kisses. The good news is, we get to choose which signals to send because our minds are as magical as the immortal genie in the bottle.

If you're unhappy with the way things are going, it's entirely possible you've been rubbing the bottle the wrong way. It might be a good idea to start looking inward to feel where the pains are coming from and then enact your own catch-and-release program, throwing back every pain that bites. Of course, if it were obvious how each nagging toothache, asthma attack, and sour stomach we suffer from is a result of the hurt, anger, and worry we carry around like an old sack lunch long after the events are over and done with, we'd decide once and for all to stop drinking victim's venom. To add insult to injury, emitting negative energy doesn't even poison the people who hurt us.

Louise Hay, author and founder of Hay House Publishing, one of the largest self-help publishers in the world, is a great example of the healing power we hold within. Louise walked away from traditional cervical cancer treatment and completely healed herself in six months by cleaning out the hurt locker she'd packed with past traumas. Her best-selling book *You Can Heal Your Life* demonstrates that everyone can heal if they let go of the past, put happiness first, and learn how to forgive others, even those who inflicted the nastiest of wounds—even when this person is themselves.

We often believe that the only way we will be loved is by showing others how much we're willing to do for them in the hopes that they'll reciprocate, but when we do things in order to feel loved and garner approval, we end up disappointed. We know we're truly happy when we put ourselves at the top of the list of the people we love. Many believe that self-love is selfish and smug, but loving ourselves genuinely is the surest way to offer the best version of ourselves to others, and it's the best chance we have of feeling love in return.

When we choose to wake up happy, chances are good our entire day will stay that way, no matter what the universe serves up. Feeling great as soon as we open our eyes automatically puts us in a better place than ninety-nine percent of the population. Once we get the hang of taking total responsibility for our thoughts and feelings, we are naturally inspired to think and act like the happy, fun loving individuals we are. Enabled to accept and work with every experience that comes up, we see setbacks as temporary and mistakes as a potential to learn new ways of thinking and doing instead of signs of gloom and doom. That's when we stop being spoofed into believing that worry and fear are prerequisites to happiness and fulfillment.

Such happiness and fulfillment are nearly tangible. People feel them. I feel them, and I found them when I found Eddie. Eddie has taught me many things, but they all culminate in this: Eddie taught me how to choose to be happy.

Every now and then, I ask Eddie why people love him so much. He shrugs playfully and answers, "I can't help it. I'm a cool guy."

Eddie chooses to be happy and comfortable in his own skin. No wonder he's come so far.

As for me, through Eddie, I have learned that happiness foreshadows every success, that every rainbow is supported by a pot of gold at both ends, and that, no matter where we live, happiness is the best place to be.

EPilogue

Let's Ride Together

At this very moment, nearly 7.5 billion people inhabit the earth. Given the numbers, it's surprising how many of us feel lonely. Even more surprising, the loneliest people live in the most highly populated and technologically advanced areas, places where they can connect at all hours and meet up to enjoy the company of others in venues ranging from coffee shops to campgrounds. With all these possibilities to meet people who would love to meet us, why do so many of us feel so alone?

The answer is simple: we have forgotten that we all sprouted from the same seedling. Living behind illusionary borders and man-made walls, we see ourselves as separate and different from one another, so we miss how innately connected we are. We choose to find reasons why we or someone else doesn't fit in, and we wear these reasons like a badge of honor. Then, as much as we don't like it when others label us, we use our perceived differences as excuses to disconnect instead of venturing out to mingle with those who might not appear to look, dress, or think like we do. We protect ourselves from getting involved so that we don't get hurt, and we avoid helping others so that we won't be judged as being like them.

It pains me to confess I initially felt apprehensive about fitting Eddie back into my life. Driving away after visiting him at Highland that first time, it would have been easy to tell myself I'd done my part and that he would be okay without me.

I ended up returning in large part because Eddie and I are so much alike. By that, I mean we're just like everyone else. We all want to be included, we all need help, we all want to help, and we all know we don't like making excuses for our failures to live up to our commitments any more than we like hearing about our failures from others.

But as much as we want to be included, most of us follow our calendars instead of our hearts when it comes to making promises to reach out. We decide we don't have time, we prioritize something else, or we save our charitable work for the holidays.

Since nothing meaningful can change without our participation, I suggest we all ignore our calendars, reach within, and extend beyond what's comfortable. We don't have to venture far to find opportunities to volunteer, and it doesn't mean we have to completely change our lives in order to make a difference in the lives of others. Like Eddie says, "You can shock the heck out of someone pretty easily." We can phone friends or relatives we haven't spoken to in years, add some coins to a parking meter, return a shopping cart, relieve a caregiver, donate a few dollars to the guy or gal holding a handmade cardboard sign, or even help out a worthy organization. When we do this, we take a step towards inclusivity.

Eddie, like the rest of us, likes to be included. One way he makes sure this happens is by regularly hosting parties. It's common for him to call to share the list of food he plans to serve at an upcoming cookout he's hosting for his friends at BrickWays plus other folks he's met at work, church, or on his daily bike rides. He loves to open his house and fire up his grill, whether it's a holiday or just an ordinary weekend. His friends show up bearing chips and pop and eagerly load up on hot dogs, hamburgers, and deviled eggs, Eddie's favorite dish to make for a crowd. They eat plenty of food but always save room for grace. When the thought strikes him, Eddie conducts a little prayer service, closing his eyes, extending his hands, and thanking God for the friends he has, asking Him to keep them safe and well.

Rest assured, Eddie is qualified to do this: he loves God fiercely, he has official business cards, and I managed to track down a clerical collar for him to wear. Most importantly, when Eddie speaks, people listen.

Today, it's incredibly rewarding to look at the beautiful landing Eddie has made on our often lonely planet. He participates in and enjoys every day. He happily reaches out to others, unafraid to build new relationships, always ready to offer his friendship without judgment. Eddie doesn't need to make life miserable or be a burden on anyone; he just wants to be free to enjoy his life on his own terms, pretty much like he enjoys his favorite shows—with as few commercial interruptions as possible.

I sometimes wonder what would have happened if Eddie and I hadn't reconnected. Even though helping him has made a difference in his life, I know he would have been happy with or without me because Eddie knows what happiness is and is keenly aware that he will never have to wait for it to come to him.

I'm the one who would have missed out on probably the greatest opportunity for personal growth, inclusion, and connection I could ever have envisioned. I'm so happy I made room in my schedule for Eddie. I'm even happier that he included me in his; but what do you expect from someone whose journey through life has always been a joyride?

"Part of the problem with the word 'disabilities' is that it immediately suggests an inability to see or hear or walk or do other things that many of us take for granted. But what of people who can't feel? Or talk about their feelings? Or manage their feelings in constructive ways? What of people who aren't able to form close and strong relationships? And people who cannot find fulfillment in their lives, or those who have lost hope, who live in disappointment and bitterness and find in life no joy, no love? These, it seems to me, are the real disabilities."

— FRED ROGERS

Eddie and Ruby at PEACE Ranch during an experiential learning class

Fast Eddie grew up in Carson City, Michigan, and has lived in Flint, Clio, Linden, Highland and Traverse City, where he now resides. While many of us spend our lifetimes finding our true purpose, Fast Eddie has been living his purpose since he was born. He knows it was no accident he was found right when he needed to be, and seemingly against all odds was whisked off to restart his life by a family that wanted and needed him. Eddie is forever thankful for the good manners his mother taught him. His enthusiasm for experiencing joy throughout his life has inspired so many people to laugh, to give and to appreciate on a whole different level. Eddie witnesses miracles every day, because he is receptive to the belief that everything is a miracle. He continues his daily routine of bike riding in Traverse City, collecting returnable bottles and cans, smiling at babies like he's running for political office and watching his favorite TV heroes mimic his best moves.

About The Author

Karen Wiand came from a big family in the little town of Carson City, Michigan, where she spent her early years fully invested in having fun with her siblings and neighbors playing hockey until her feet were frozen on their annual rink constructed by their father, sneaking past No Trespassing signs to investigate abandoned barns and houses in a full out search for ghosts or jumping in the car at moment's notice when her dad took them on mystery road trips. The family home doubled as the neighborhood clubhouse and the door was always open. The attitude of inclusion instilled by her parents has helped her throughout her life, and she has used those principles to accept and appreciate that every life is precious and every perspective matters. She continues to advocate for and learn from Eddie and his friends, and marvels at how large his family has become. Hardly a day goes by in Traverse City without someone he met years ago and miles away shouting from across the street or tapping him on the shoulder with an emphatic, "Is that you, Fast Eddie?"

You can learn more about Fast Eddie and Karen at
karenwiand.com.